13-Digit ISBN: 978-1-40034-094-1

10-Digit ISBN: 1-40034-094-2

This book may be ordered by mail from the publisher. Please include $5.99 for postage and handling. Please support your local bookseller first!

Books published by Cider Mill Press Book Publishers are available at special discounts for bulk purchases in the United States by corporations, institutions, and other organizations. For more information, please contact the publisher.

Cider Mill Press Book Publishers
"Where good books are ready for press"
501 Nelson Place
Nashville, Tennessee 37214
cidermillpress.com

Typography: Meno Text, HWT Aetna

Image Credits: Pages 8–9, 18, 44, 52, 74–75, 188–189, 195, 221, 225, 226, 236–237, 269, and 270–271 courtesy of Unsplash. Pages 23, 90–91, 103, 106–107, 110–111, 120–121, 123, and 144–145 courtesy of Cider Mill Press. Front cover courtesy of Shutterstock. All other photos courtesy of the author.

Printed in Malaysia

24 25 26 27 28 OFF 5 4 3 2 1

First Edition

WHISKEY STORIES

STORIES

THE TRUE SPIRIT BEHIND THE LABELS

RICHARD THOMAS

CIDER MILL PRESS

BOOK
PUBLISHERS

CONTENTS

FOREWORD
By Neal Thompson

What you're about to read is a wonderful and eclectic collection—a journey, really, from the backroads of Bluegrass Country to the Scottish Isles to Ireland and Japan—as Richard Thomas takes us behind the scenes at the world's most famous distilleries, sharing the stories and secrets of your favorite whiskeys, and mine.

In these pages, you'll gain a new perspective on the techniques and traditions that go into distilling, aging, and blending the whiskeys of today, and what went into those produced in the past. You'll gain (or expand) an appreciation of the heritage and history, the charm and craftsmanship of the ancient science of whiskey making. Mainly, you'll enjoy colorful tales and curious bits of historical ephemera, ammunition to share with friends over drinks. Do you know who that man is striding across the Johnnie Walker bottle? Do you know how and why Maker's Mark is sealed with red wax? Do you know the role Irish independence played in the history of Jamesons? Where Four Roses got its name? By the end of these pages, you'll know all that and more.

As someone who's written about the history of whiskey in America, I considered myself a student of the water of life's journey from Scotland and Ireland to the states, of corn liquor's evolution from moonshine to Maker's. But I was surprised at how much I learned here—about the ex-moonshiners turned pot farmers of Marion County, Kentucky. About the four Ws of Maker's Mark and the history of that red wax seal. About the near death of Four Roses and other American whiskeys, pulled back from the brink by the Bourbon Boom.

As whiskey tourism has soared—in America, it put Kentucky's Bourbon Trail on a global map—whiskey, bourbon, and Scotch distilleries have become destinations, glass-and-steel showplaces whose museum-like facades and stunningly designed tasting rooms front the labs, factories, and warehouses where the real action happens. This is where Thomas's curiosity thrives, as he heads deep into the nooks and crannies where the magic happens, behind the facades where we meet the men and women who've devoted their lives to this craft. This is a master class on how today's amber liquor gets made, and the love that goes into it. And it's an homage to the hard work, entrepreneurship, ingenuity, love, and passion that goes into each bottle.

In the pages ahead you'll meet indelibly colorful characters, from Shinto priests and ghosts to George Orwell. You'll witness at least one murder and a good bit of mayhem. Mainly you'll get to know the devoted people whose recipes, hacks, ricks, stillhouses, and family traditions beautifully mesh into a story of craftsmanship and creativity. It'll make you appreciate that next sip in a whole new way.

PREFACE

One theme presented itself time and again as I researched this book—that making whiskey attracts outsized personalities. There is a storytelling aspect that goes with making certain drinks, whether it be wine or beer or mezcal. Tales are in the air when one sits down for a guided tasting or bellies up to the right bar, where the bartenders know their salt. Yet I feel there is something special about the people who make whiskey, a singular quality in the whiskey trade itself. Perhaps it is the deep, mature character of the drink or that its proper maturation requires a minimum of several years of patient aging. But whatever the reason, whiskey culture is associated with big characters and tall tales.

The same can be said of the people who drink it. The Google, AI-derived answer to "what kind of person drinks whiskey," is a mature, confident person who enjoys complexity in their drinking. This is the rare instance when I won't argue that the AI answer is a stupid one. I enjoy a good beer, a fine glass of wine (I spend no small amount of money on Port these days), and lean on gin when the steamy Kentucky summer rolls around, but I just don't find the same kind of people at a tap-house or a winery that I do at a bourbon club event or at a dedicated whiskey bar. It's a tribe that, as I have discovered, has some pretty good stories of its own to tell.

My own whiskey story began in 1988. My father was a thor-oughbred horse breeder and had recently bought a larger farm on the border of Woodford and Franklin counties in Kentucky. I was already becoming quite outdoorsy, and the move coin-cided with my learning to drive and acquiring a car, so I got out a map and studied my new environs. I found a feature not far away called Glenn's Creek. The area looked pretty remote, so I reckoned I may find a good perch for wildlife watching. I drove over to Millville, parked the car, and went exploring McCracken Pike on my bicycle, looking for a way to access Glenn's Creek itself without getting shot at by a farmer (in 1980s' Kentucky, that meant a shotgun packed with rock salt).

What I found, tucked behind chain-link fences and other bar-riers, was one place that looked like an old factory and two other separate complexes of grander yet more rundown build-ings. The factory was the Old Crow Distillery. One of the dilapidated structures still had a sign that read "The Old Tay-lor Distilling Company." The other, I would later learn, was the Labrot & Graham Distillery. I set about doing what today is called urban exploring, but in Reagan's America was plain old trespassing.

In the 1980s, the bourbon industry wasn't the source of Kentucky pride that it is today. When I stumbled into Old Taylor, the business was still mired in the aftermath of a major downturn in the 1970s, one that had forced Old Crow to shut down just the year before I found it. The state was also full of teetotaling "dries," people who abhorred alcohol (although they were happy enough to use taxes on the bourbon industry to fund their sheriff and fire departments), and bourbon was largely perceived as a blue-collar, down-market drink, the curious marketing of Maker's Mark notwithstanding. The advertising on billboards in Louisville and Lexington promoted Crown Royal, not local bourbon.

The existence of the bourbon industry was just plain ignored as I was growing up, at least in the circles I lived in. The only time I ever heard it spoken about was when people were left scratching their heads at why on earth Maker's Mark would want to sell whiskey to the Japanese or Australians, a question prompted by something they read in the local paper. This was hardly the only part of my upbringing that turned out to be very wrongheaded about local affairs. The Civil War received a similar neglect, as I was told throughout my school years that not much happened in Kentucky beyond one minor, indecisive battle. Unless the subject was Daniel Boone, there wasn't much heritage being shared in the Kentucky of those days, and what little was being shared was often wrong.

But one only needed to look at the timeworn fieldstone building at Labrot & Graham or the ruined, Angkor-like grandeur of Old Taylor to realize there was something special about this industry, something intrinsically Kentucky, but nobody I knew seemed to care about it. I began to ask why, and soon discovered another ruined titan of the Kentucky bourbon industry that was close to a former home. Two miles up Viley Road from my father's first farm was the ruin of the James E. Pepper Distillery. We would drive past it in his Chevy truck, either to fetch sub sandwiches or visit with my uncle, who worked at Kings Foods (also set in what had been old bourbon warehouses). That mammoth complex sitting alongside Town Branch had captured my boyhood imagination. In my late teens, I returned to the site armed with the knowledge of its history.

I spent the next several years, as I found the time, looking into where working and shuttered distilleries were and visiting the grounds. But I was also an outward-looking youth. My first trip out of the US was to England, when I was eighteen. I went to a bar, properly legal to drink in that country, and began trying Scotch to the limits of my meager budget.

My teenage self soon realized that what I was being told by adults back home about Kentucky and its whiskey didn't reflect the truth. By the time I had moved to Washington, DC, and enrolled in graduate school, one of those distilleries on McCracken Pike was already out of my reach for further exploration. On a visit home, I could see Brown-Forman was up to something at the old Labrot & Graham place. By 1996, that something was revealed as Woodford Reserve.

People were beginning to talk about bourbon again, too. I remember one woman I dated briefly who, I was surprised to discover, was very into Knob Creek, and without my having to introduce her to it. The liquor store one block over from my apartment was owned by an African American family, and their enterprising son was trying to make it more upscale, to reflect our (scarcely) gentrifying neighborhood. He always had one bottle of Blanton's out on the top shelf, and when I asked him why it was always just the one bottle, he told me, "The bottle is pretty and the stopper is pretty, and sitting there all by itself, it says 'I'm special' to people. So, they buy it, and I put out another." But he didn't know anything about how Blanton's had come to be in the decade before.

What follows are stories about whiskey, its people, places, and methods, with a lot of "how things got to be this way" for good measure. These are tales of rogues, entrepreneurs, crafty folks, blue-collar workers and scientists in pursuit of triumph and suffering calamity. This book is written by an American and will reach a largely American audience, so it is very America-centric, but I was thrilled to be able to spend some time with the world's other major whiskey-making regions: Canada, Ireland, Japan, and Scotland.

Women occupy a growing and leading role in making whiskey today, but that was hardly the case before the 21st century, apart from Margaret Samuels. Knowing that I would spend a lot of time writing about long dead white men, I made a choice to help balance the scales by writing only two types of biographical profiles for this book: the industry's living legends and the young women already holding top whiskey-making spots at their respective companies. The former all played key roles in delivering the whiskey industry to where it is today, while the latter are going to carry it forward (hopefully) for the next 20 to 30 years.

Recent years have also seen more attention paid to the untold story of African Americans working in the American whiskey industry. Nathan "Nearest" Green is the most famous of these, but only that: the most famous. Just how integral the expertise of enslaved distillery workers was to the early history of whiskey making in the Upper South is a story only now being understood and told. Hand in glove with that increased understanding are how other African Americans are claiming that legacy and taking ownership of their own whiskey enterprises.

On that regional note, I should address a tedious and most pedantic point of spelling, whether the term is "whisky" or "whiskey." The general rule is that whenever the term is used in a specific reference, it follows the spelling of that reference, so Caol Ila whisky or Early Times whiskey, for example. But whenever I'm referring to the drink in general terms, it's whiskey. Most people won't care which way I spell it, and those who do care will probably ignore that I'm obeying the mandate of a style guide. The irony is that it's the latter who make the explanation necessary.

All that said, cheers!

INTRODUCTION

Describing a drink like cider or wine as a product of natural processes is an easy reach, because all one needs to do is crush the fruit, let natural yeast in the air do its thing, and you've got alcoholic fruit. It might not be palatable, but you've got a basic version of those drinks, and it's thought that our very ability to consume alcohol without dying is an adaptation to that reality: it allowed our ancient, pre-human ancestors to eat slightly boozy, starting-to-turn-rotten fruit.

Yet as often as the natural side of whiskey gets emphasized, making whiskey is as much about industry as anything else. That is because it is rooted in distillation, which is a surprisingly ancient, yet technical process. Aristotle wrote about it in his *Meteorology*, when he described "vaporizing" seawater to remove the salt, and archeological finds indicate people might have been distilling things as early as 3,500 BCE.

Distillation is the science of separating compounds by exploiting their different vaporization points, or the temperature at which they boil off. In Aristotle's example, the purpose is to make the water evaporate and leave behind the salt. This process is used in salt pans to produce sea salt and solar stills to produce drinkable water. Water boils at 212°F, while salt boils at 2,669°F (almost hot enough to melt iron), so separating the two is simple, requiring only a little sunshine and a bowl.

The Chinese are known to have been distilling a spirit from fermented rice as far back as 800 BCE. Although rice whiskey is a thing, China's proto-baijiu isn't thought of as the earliest whiskey. For that, we need to look to Ireland and Scotland. Who came first is anyone's guess, and both have written references dating to the 15th century. Those early written records refer to *aqua vitae*, Latin for the "water of life." The term in Irish is *uisce beatha*, and in Gaelic it is the slightly different *uisge beatha*. This late medieval and Renaissance era spirit was an unaged whiskey, and often flavored with fruit or herbs. My guess is the drink around today tasting most like this ancient form of whiskey is genever. The difference lies in that genever is infused with herbs as it is being made, while the recipes for making that early, unaged whiskey drinkable called for adding them after. What the Irish and Scots were doing with their whiskeys before the middle of the 19th century is, in fact, reminiscent of what American moonshiners often do with their hooch today.

Before moving on, it's important to define what makes whiskey, whiskey. I've met people at festivals in Scotland who claim anything that isn't spelled "whisky" doesn't count, and folks at bourbon events who say bourbon isn't whiskey at all. Both claims are wrong, because wherever and however it is made, all whiskey has one rudimentary, but necessary characteristic:

Whiskey is fermented from grain. If anything else is used as a sugar source or flavoring element while making the actual alcohol, it isn't whiskey.

The point of whiskey is to retain some of the native flavor of the grain from which it is made. Gin and vodka can also be made from grain, but because they are distilled to a higher strength of alcohol, the native spirit is close to or entirely odorless and tasteless.

Each national tradition is already the subject of many books. So, the purpose of what follows is not a comprehensive study, but simply a starting point. If you think I've sacrificed too much to brevity, she can be a cruel mistress, and I invite you to come find me and start a conversation on the subject of comparative whiskey nerd-dom.

HOW WHISKEY GETS MADE

The simplest way to describe how whiskey is made is this: take some beer and distill it, in much the same way that distilling wine or cider yields brandy. Just as in beer, the process starts by simmering ground grain in water to make a mash. This breaks down and/or dissolves starches, oils, and proteins in the grain in preparation for fermentation. Alcohol, of course, is made by fermenting sugar. Fruit has a lot of inherent sugar, but grain doesn't. What grain has is a lot of starch, so enzymes need to be present in the mash to convert the starch to sugar. This is why beer and whiskey both start with malted barley because malted barley contains the necessary enzymes.

Once a distiller has a sugary mash, it can be fermented by yeast. Ask any baker and they will tell you the strain of yeast is at least as important to how the bread will turn out as the choice of flour. Likewise, yeast contributes to the flavors found in beer and whiskey; the banana note found in Old Forester and Jack Daniel's comes from their yeasts, both made by their parent company, Brown-Forman. Once the yeast has done its work, the mash can be distilled to separate the alcohol spirit from the slurry of water and grain.

Whiskey distillers use three basic types of stills. There are actually many variants and charmingly anachronistic designs in use today, but to keep it simple and brief, the world industry

relies on pot stills, column stills, and hybrid stills. Pot stills are the antique design and consist of a pot with a tube sticking out the top, which bends back into a condenser. The pot is heated to a point where the alcohol will vaporize, leaving most of the water and any solids behind. The vapor rises up to the top to collect in the condenser, where it turns back into a liquid and flows out of the system. Pot stills usually require two or three rounds of distillation to achieve the desired strength of alcohol, which is why the stills are often arranged in sets.

The column still is an invention of the industrial revolution, perfected by Aeneas Coffey in 1832. The column has perforated plates inserted throughout its length, and the operating concept is to let steam rise from the bottom while pouring mash in from the top. As the steam rises, the alcohol is vaporized while the water condenses, cools, and drips back down to the bottom, and any material that collects at the bottom is drained. As in a pot still, alcohol vapor rises out through the top, where it can be collected and condensed back into liquid. The main advantage of the column still is that it can be operated continuously, whereas pot stills must run in batches.

Hybrid stills are a common sight with small distilleries, and, as the name implies, are a cross between the two. A typical hybrid has a pot as its base, crowned with a small column. Although a hybrid cannot operate continuously, the column functions as a second still bolted onto the pot, as it were, so the company doesn't need to have a set of pot stills.

Copper is preferred because the metal reacts with certain unwanted, volatile compounds released in the distillation process, removing them from the vapor. That is one of the reasons why stills gradually wear out and require regular maintenance; the reaction eats away at the copper. Copper is also a soft metal, so using it in industrial machinery tends to give it a short working life, compared to, say, using it in your kitchenware. Stainless steel and combinations of stainless steel and copper are also used in making stills.

Once the alcohol spirit has been distilled to the desired strength, it is a "new make" whiskey. Maturation in oak casks follows, but that has only been the case since the 19th century. Before that, aging in wood was not the norm, which is why new make whiskey was routinely moderated with the addition of fruit, herbs, and spices.

Maturation is how a whiskey acquires half or more (often much more) of its odor and flavor, as well as all its color. It's a dance between the species of oak (and sometimes even where the oak was grown), the size of the cask and how much it has been used prior to being filled with whiskey, the climate of where the whiskey is matured, and sometimes even where the cask sits in a given warehouse. Put a whiskey in a first-fill sherry butt, leave it in a dunnage warehouse in the Speyside region of Scotland for twenty years, and you'll come away with a lovely batch of single malt. Fill a barrel of charred new white oak with bourbon and put that on the top floor of a five-story rickhouse in Shively for the same twenty years, and you'll come away with a couple of gallons or less of dreadfully over-oaked whiskey.

Just how complicated maturation is escapes many drinkers, who tend to focus simply on the number of years indicated on the bottle. What is too often forgotten is the expertise of those making the whiskey over the course of those years.

WHISKEY MAKING
IN THE UNITED STATES

As anyone who has ever been on a Kentucky bourbon distillery tour knows, bourbon is made with 51 percent or more corn. This point, enforced by federal whiskey law, underlines the first feature that separates American whiskey making from the rest of the world: the mash bill. American whiskey tends to be made with a recipe of two or more grains and is defined by whatever its lead grain is. Thus, bourbon is mostly corn, rye whiskey is mostly rye, and so on. The four major types—bourbon, rye, wheat, and malt whiskeys—are required to have 51 percent or more of the lead grain. One of the traits that differentiates corn whiskey from bourbon is that it is overwhelmingly made from corn, 80 percent or more.

In recent years, a movement has taken off to give the American Single Malt the force of law. When this new definition is enshrined into federal regulations, it will create two separate categories. The American Malt, as it already exists with 51 percent malted barley in the mash, and the American Single Malt, made to correspond with single malt standards as they exist internationally: the latter will also be allowed to mature in both used and new barrels. But for now, the terminology can be confusing, so just be aware that if you see an American malt whiskey, it might not be a true single malt directly comparable to, say, The Glenfarclas. Woodford Reserve Malt is not comparable, to cite just one example, because it is made with 51 percent malted barley.

An odd feature is that Americans use mash, while most of the rest of the world use wort and wash. The difference is mash keeps the solids in for the entire process. As just explored, the Irish-Scottish model takes the solids out to create the wort. Whenever I've asked about this, I've been told either "I don't know why we/they do it that way" or else that keeping the grain solids in the mash imparts wanted/unwanted flavors to the distillate. Sometimes I am told, and I believe this is the true answer, that the column still separates the solids out on its own and is, to a degree, self-cleaning. A pot still must be cleaned after each run, a job that is laborious if it has a crust of solids at the bottom. Until the craft whiskey sector arose after 2005, American whiskey makers relied on column stills, so they could afford to work with mash instead of wash.

That raises the next distinctive feature of American whiskey: it doesn't matter what kind of still is used in making it. No legal category, style, or regional tradition is dependent on a particular make or model of still in the way that malt whiskey must be made in a pot still, and grain whiskey must be made in a column still. Big distillers prefer column stills (although Woodford Reserve runs an Irish-style triple set of pot stills), while small and medium-sized producers might use columns, pots, or hybrids, depending on their means and aims.

The final distinctive feature is reliance on new oak maturation. The four major categories I just outlined all require maturation in new oak barrels. Not all American whiskeys must be so aged; the co-feature that distinguishes corn whiskey from bourbon, apart from its overwhelming corn content, is that it must be aged in used oak barrels. Early Times is a so-called "Kentucky Whiskey," and is essentially what could have been a bourbon new make, except that it's aged in used barrels. Still, four out of five bottles of premium American whiskey made today are either bourbon or rye, and that should tell you about the primacy of new oak maturation in the American tradition.

WHISKY MAKING IN CANADA

Canada is the outlier of the five traditional whiskey-making nations. No one has adopted either the American or Canadian models, but the American whiskey industry is a peer of the Scotch industry, both worth approximately $8.5 billion in annual sales. It could therefore be said (and it is also a very American thing to say) that America is a giant all on its own and doesn't *need* anyone to adopt its model to make it great. Ireland and Japan are part of the same family as Scotland. Canada is both relatively small *and* unique.

Canadian whisky is synonymous with rye, and rye is the predominate grain used to make Canadian whisky, but it can be made from any grain. A distinctive aspect of the Canadian whisky industry is how each individual grain type is milled, mashed, fermented, distilled, and matured separately. So, in a Canadian warehouse one will find corn, rye, wheat, and malt whiskies, giving the company making it a palette of whiskies to blend together in making their products.

Canadian companies also make these one-grain spirits in two broad types: as either base or flavoring whiskies. Base whiskies are the foundation of the product, especially in mass market Canadian whiskies. A base whisky is usually made from corn, but wheat or rye may be used. It is distilled to a high proof (180 to 190 proof, almost vodka) and aged in a used cask, making it a light spirit that is cheaper to produce. It has some similarities in production style and intent as grain whiskey has in the Irish-Scottish model. Flavoring whiskies are distilled to a lower proof in either a column or pot still (or even both) and aged in either used or new oak casks. This painter's palette approach influenced certain distilleries that in America were once owned by the defunct Canadian conglomerate Seagram, such as MGP in Indiana and Four Roses in Kentucky.

In common with Ireland and Scotland, but definitely not the United States, Canadian law says that anything called Canadian whisky must be aged for a minimum of three years. Finally, Canadian whiskies may contain up to 9.09 percent additives for either flavoring or coloring, although one often doesn't see that except in the cheapest of products.

AN OVERVIEW OF WHISKEY MAKING OUTSIDE OF NORTH AMERICA

Whiskey making has spread widely in the 21st century, from South Africa and Mexico to Australia and Taiwan. With very few exceptions, those newcomers have adopted the same model for making whiskey (or whisky, as the Scots and most of the rest of the world prefer) developed by the Irish and Scots. The Japanese were the first to adapt that model and build a distinctive national industry with it. That means three of the world's five major whiskey-making nations and almost all of its minor ones use a similar production process.

The core of this model is its original form, malt whiskey. Malted barley is cooked as described, and the solids are filtered out. The liquid that remains is called wort, which is fermented. After fermentation, the liquid is called wash, and the wash goes to distillation in pot stills.

The second format is grain whiskey, which came about with the development of the column still, because the column still tends to make a lighter whiskey. This form uses a variety of grains in making the wort, not just barley. Corn, wheat, rye, and rice all appear in grain whiskey; Girvan, which makes grain whisky for William Grant & Sons, uses a recipe of 10 percent malted barley and 90 percent wheat.

For both malt and grain whiskeys, the new distillate is placed in a variety of cask types for maturation, and almost all of them are used casks. The Irish and Scots came to rely on used casks because their lands are heavily deforested. Ireland and the Netherlands are tied as the most deforested countries in Europe; Scotland is only slightly better off, and the two Celtic nations have been that way for centuries. There is so little mature native oak around to use for barrels that it's noteworthy when a whiskey is made with it, as is the case for Middleton Dair Ghaelach, which tells you exactly what tree and what wood lot the new Irish oak cask came from.

Their industries became dependent on repurposed barrels, initially from European wine industries and then from the American whiskey industry. Ex-bourbon and Tennessee whiskey wood stock predominates in the Irish, Japanese, and Scotch industries, with former fortified wine casks (sherry, Port, Madeira, etc.) running a distant second by numbers, and a smattering of other types (rum, virgin new oak, etc.) making up the difference.

Once I saw master distiller Fred Noe on a panel with some colleagues from Scottish and Irish distilleries that were all owned by what was then Beam Global (before Suntory bought the company in 2014), and he was asked if his bourbon was better than their Scotch. He said, "Well, I get a new oak barrel and use it up, and when I'm done with it, I give it to these fellers. Make of that what you will." Noe's good-natured jibe underlines the role of the ex-bourbon barrel in whiskey making in Scotland, Ireland, Japan, and everywhere else.

In 1999, Heaven Hill was selling 75,000 used bourbon barrels to Scotland alone; today that number is 80 percent of their total barrel dumps per year. Exactly how many barrels Heaven Hill is dumping nowadays isn't public information, but they are known to run one of the largest distilleries in Kentucky 24 hours a day, seven days a week for approximately 320 days a year, for an output of approximately 400,000 barrels per annum. The company is also sitting on top of the second largest inventory of aging bourbon in the state. Looking at numbers like that from a Scottish perspective, nine out of ten casks used in the Scotch industry today are either ex-bourbon barrels or hogsheads (a somewhat larger barrel type) built from the staves of old bourbon barrels.

These casks, rebuilt and refinished by coopers after each batch, can be used over and over again. A first-fill barrel is therefore quite prized, because the oak still has some of its native flavors left, and the influence of whatever was previously matured in it lingers on. By the time a cask gets to its third or fourth fill, it is little more than a breathable container. Even countries that have a thriving lumber industry tend to mature their whiskey using old barrels because they follow the Irish and Scottish model. It is part of the three-legged stool of the Irish and Scottish production model: malt whiskey, grain whiskey, and old casks.

Some of the mature whiskeys are released as single malt and single grain whiskeys (unblended and made at one distillery), but the vast majority of the output in Ireland, Japan, and Scotland goes into blended whiskeys, a mixture of the two. To put the relative scale of these types into perspective, The Glenfiddich has been the top-selling single malt Scotch brand for all but a couple of years, when The Glenlivet briefly nudged it aside before slipping back to second place. The 1.2 million cases it sold in 2021, however, put the best-selling single malt in only 19th place among the top 20 Scotch brands. By far the dominant whiskey coming out of Ireland is a blend, Jameson, and the best-selling whiskey in the world of any description is Johnnie Walker, also a blend.

THE GIANTS OF JAPANESE WHISKY

M any, many hands went into making the whiskey industries we recognize in Scotland, Ireland, the United States, and Canada. Although some folks still believe the fable that Elijah Craig single-handedly invented Kentucky bourbon (see page 127), most realize that these things are about dozens of businessmen, chemists, and distillers making individual contributions, layering up the knowledge and sense of identity.

Then there is Japan. Just two men were instrumental in the creation of Japanese whisky as we know it today: Shinjiro Torii and Masataka Taketsuru.

Torii was born in Osaka in 1879, in what was the middle of the rapid modernization and revival of imperial rule of the Meiji Restoration. He became a pharmacist's apprentice, and working for a pharmacological wholesaler in his teens made him familiar with Western-style spirits. As was the case with many pharmacists and grocers in Scotland at approximately the same time, Torri began exploring the art of blending. By 1899, he had set up the Torii Shoten store and launched a brand of sweet wine, but that was just a start. What Torri lacked in formal training, he made up for with his sensory prowess, and back in the day he was dubbed "the nose" (Richard Patterson of The Dalmore bears the same title in the Scotch industry today). His real ambition was to make Scotch-style whiskies in Japan.

Taketsuru was younger, born in 1894 in Hiroshima, and came from a family with business roots in brewing sake. From that background, he went to work for a Japanese liquor company, trained there as a chemist, and one of his early tasks was making (cheaper) spirits that looked and tasted like imported whisky. He was also one of the few people available who spoke English, a rare skill in Japan in the World War I era. This led him to being dispatched by his employers to study whisky making in Scotland.

He began with a chemistry course at the University of Glasgow in 1918, and then interned with the Longmorn and Bo'Ness distilleries in 1919. By the time he returned to Japan in 1920, he had married a Scotswoman, Rita Cowan.

In the meantime, Taketsuru's employers had been forced by deteriorating economic circumstances to abandon their plans to open up the Japanese whisky industry. That is how Taket-suru, the only man in Japan with firsthand knowledge of the Scotch industry, found himself working for Shinjiro Torii. The pair would build the Yamazaki Distillery, Japan's first malt distillery, in 1923.

Torii's company would become known as Suntory. Officially, Suntory is a play on the sun plus the word for Shinto gates, *torii*, which is also the founder's own name (the two words have different spellings in kanji, though). Unofficially, it's said the name comes from the locals and workers of Yamazaki constantly greeting the company founder with "Torri-san," which inspired "San-tory."

Yamazaki's first whisky, a single malt called Shirofada ("white label") was a failure, and Taketsuru found himself working in a Torii-owned brewery in Yokohama. Waiting out his 10-year contract, Taketsuru struck out on his own. As it happened, Rita had been teaching English to the wife of a businessman in Yamazaki, Shotaro Kaga, and Kaga would later be an important financier of Taketsuru's Yoichi Distillery. The distillery opened with a single still in 1934, initially making apple brandy. The whisky finally came in 1936. Taketsuru's company would become Nikka.

One cannot imagine Japanese whisky today without its two goliaths, Suntory and Nikka, so it is just as hard to imagine it without both Torri and Taketsuru. Yet of the two, it is Taketsuru who is known as the "Father of Japanese Whisky," and it is not hard to see why. His fingerprints are all over both Yamazaki and Yoichi.

This is where Japan's economic culture stepped in to shape the identity of their respective whisky companies. Before the Second World War, Japan was dominated by *zaibatsu*, which could be described as a cross between a conglomerate and a cartel. After the war, that culture continued in the form of *keiretsu*, an alliance of interlocking companies centered on a common bank, which was looser and more horizontally organized than the preceding, strongly vertical zaibatsu. How this impacts Japanese whisky is that it illustrates the Japanese practice of trying to keep everything in-house, or at least in-keiretsu.

Scotland has a sprawling industry, which even at its smallest had several dozen distilleries owned by several separate companies, and these readily traded whisky stocks with each other to create their blends. Post-Prohibition, the American industry was more centralized, but also featured stock trading between companies. In Japan, Nikka and Suntory have never done mutual business in this cooperative way, and they never will. If either company needs something they don't have, say a whisky with a particular flavor profile, they develop it in-house or else build a new house and make it there. So, Suntory's Yamazaki doesn't have rows of pot stills, in the way that most Scottish distilleries do, all working in harmony to produce identical distillate. Instead, this one distillery has a diverse slate of pot still designs, something one can see at a glance. If that slate isn't sufficient to produce the flavor profiles Suntory needs, then the company also owns Hakushu (which makes grain and malt whiskies) and Chita (making grain whisky only). This trio better resembles a Midleton or a big distiller in Kentucky rather than a Glenlivet or Macallan in its scope of operation.

The same applies to Nikka, which also owns Miyagikyo (which makes malt and grain whiskies). Nikka has its idiosyncratic Miyagikyo grain whisky, which is made from a rarely used, all malted barley recipe. In an anachronistic touch, Yoichi continues to use coal fires to directly heat their stills, the only distillery in the world to do so (although Barton 1792 in Kentucky also burns coal, this is to heat their boilers, so the still is actually steam-heated).

Even Mars Whisky, a much smaller player compared to Nikka or Suntory, opened a second distillery to create a separate slate of flavor profiles from the original. In Japanese whisky, autarky—or self-reliance, if you prefer—is the signature production strategy.

Perhaps the most interesting quirk of Japanese whisky is that there was no legal or regulatory regime governing what it was and how it was made until 2021. Compare this to the Scotch industry, which is governed by a clear British law and their trade organization, the Scotch Whisky Association. Exploiting this lack of standards, some Japanese whisky companies incorporated whiskies imported from outside of Japan and other Japanese nonwhisky spirits into their products, although the big two of Nikka and Suntory have never been known to do this.

What happened in 2021 wasn't a new law, but instead a set of guidelines from Japan's own liquor trade group, the Japanese Spirits & Liqueurs Makers Association. The transitional grace period came to an end on March 31, 2024. After that, a new set of standards similar to those in Ireland and Scotland went into effect, and consumers will be sure that if they buy a non-Nikka or -Suntory brand, it will be all whisky and all Japanese.

THE WHISKY WAR

The Whisky War wasn't much of a war, due in large measure to its participants being two of the nicest nations on the planet: Canada and Denmark. Nonetheless, it was a very real territorial dispute, of the type that might have ended in shooting if it had not been between peoples who enjoy a friendly drink.

Hans Island lies in the Kennedy Channel, between Greenland (a Danish autonomous territory) and the indisputably Canadian Ellesmere Island. It is a small, barren rock, but both countries claim it. In 1984, Canadian soldiers disembarked on the island, planted their red maple leaf banner, and left a bottle of whisky sitting next to it. That bottle has been often depicted as Canadian Club, but I've never read any definitive testimony as to what, exactly, the brand of that first bottle of the Whisky War was.

Denmark's Minister of Greenland Affairs, Tom Høyem, came in person to Hans Island later that same year. He had the Danish flag put up, sat a bottle of schnapps next to it, and left a note underneath reading "Welcome to this Danish island."

For the next four decades, Canada and Denmark would have a variety of official reasons to send expeditions to the island. Some of these were scientific and some military, but the pattern was generally to take down the other side's stuff, put up a new flag plus maybe a plaque or cairn, and leave a bottle of booze. The Canadians invariably chose whisky. There were proposals to share the island, but these came to nothing until 2022. Prompted by the Russian invasion of Ukraine, the two countries decided to end the dispute, with an eye on demonstrating how diplomatic means can resolve territorial wrangling. Canada and Denmark have agreed to divide the lonely island, much to the dismay of anyone on official business in the Kennedy Channel. Such folks no longer have that free bottle of booze to look forward to.

THE GRIST OF BEER
AND WHISKEY

Barley is a cornerstone grain of both brewing and whiskey making, even in traditions like bourbon, which is primarily made from corn. This is because, once malted, barley releases enzymes that convert the starch in the various grains to sugar, and it is the sugar that is later fermented into alcohol. In American whiskey making, a little malted barley goes a long way, unlocking the potential of the corn, wheat, and rye. In Scotland, Japan, and many other places, the most prized whiskies are made entirely from malted barley.

Malting is controlled germination. Grains are seeds, and the point of malting is to get the seeds to begin sprouting, and then to halt that process. The barley is moistened with water and, once germination has taken place, air-dried. The malted barley is then stored for future use.

Most distillers buy their malt from commercial vendors, but some still make it themselves, which invariably means that the distiller is engaged in the quaint practice of floor malting. This method dates to Roman times, and those who employ it are either passionate about tradition or have a punk rock, DIY ethos. Or both.

The barley is steeped in water and then spread out on a concrete, tile, or stone floor with a specialized wood rake. Germination will take four or five days, during which time the grain must be turned about with a scoop shovel three times a day to prevent the grains from sprouting their roots. If that happens, the malt is said to have formed a "mat." Floor malting is labor-intensive, which is why most distillers source their malted barley from a commercial malting company, where the process is mechanized.

Several distilleries in Scotland never ceased floor malting, among them Balvenie, BenRiach, Bowmore, Highland Park, Lagavulin, Laphroaig, and Springbank. Yet this backbreaking, romantic practice isn't limited to just Scotland. As some American craft distillers have dedicated themselves to producing single malts, a few have likewise adopted floor malting, such as Arizona's Del Bac, Colorado's Leopold Brothers, and Virginia's Copper Fox. It helps that many small distillers in

America got their first experience in making liquor in brewing, which has its own floor malting tradition. Internationally, Japan's Chichibu and Denmark's Stauning are among other whisky makers malting their own barley.

As floor malting for whiskey has gone worldwide, some aspects have been adapted to the new locales. Smoky single malt Scotch is very much a knock-on effect of the floor malting process. To heat those chilly Scottish malting chambers, the Scots had to burn something, and peat was often the cheapest fuel available. Thick peat smoke would permeate the room, leaving its imprint on the grain and thereby finding its way into the whisky.

Different locales, different fuels. In the southwestern United States, it has become a regional signature to smoke grain using mesquite wood, which has long been a fixture of the region's barbecue. When a distiller is doing their own floor maltings *and* burning mesquite to heat the room, as Del Bac does, they've taken a process all the way from Islay or Dufftown and made it their own.

THE PROOF IS IN THE FLAME

Two things differentiate whiskeys made in the United States from those made anywhere else, and neither of them is how the word "whiskey" is spelled. Although this is starting to change, American whiskeys come in 750 ml "fifth" bottles, and the strength of the alcohol inside it leads with the measurement in proof. For most of the globe, that bottle is 700 ml and the measurement is in alcohol by volume (ABV). In keeping with their distinctive style, Canada does both.

As a modern reference, proof is double the ABV. Whiskey everywhere is at least 40 percent ABV, which translates to 80 proof. As many a distillery tour guide has been asked, if that is how the two measurements work, why use proof at all? The answer is that whiskey as a trade has a love for its anachronisms, and the term dates back to an era before the instruments needed to precisely measure ABV had been invented yet.

Proof harkens back to 16th century England, when the crown placed an extra tax on "proof spirits," which had stronger alcohol content. That proof came from a test performed by soaking gunpowder in the liquor and then trying to light that gunpowder on fire. If it could be lit to burning, but didn't explode in a flash, then it was proof that the spirits were strong enough to be more heavily taxed. The fault in this system was the air temperature was also a variable in whether the alcohol-soaked gunpowder could be lit. Contrary to myth, 100 proof isn't the threshold for when alcohol-moistened gunpowder will burn.

The trifecta of fire, booze, and gunpowder appears on every 14-year-old boy's vision board, but in 1816 the British government grew up and established specific gravity as the new means of determining proof. That proof, again for tax purposes, was formally set at 57.06 percent ABV.

In typical fashion, the United States simplified this system. In 1848, the US government established the rule that proof is double the ABV, and then set the threshold for "proof spirits" (again, a taxation thing) at 100 proof.

Being the home of the metric system, the French came up with their own system for determining a proof spirit. Their system puts ABV and proof on a 1-for-1 ratio, so in their system 100 proof equals 100 percent alcohol. Keeping in mind that you can substitute alcohol for gasoline pretty well at 95 percent ABV, 100 proof liquor in France burns with or without the gunpowder.

WOOD STOCK (NEITHER THE CONCERT NOR THE BIRD)

The story of whiskey and wood is actually two stories. First is the one often heard on distillery tours, and that is the story of barrel maturation: the complicated dance between the oak of the cask, time, and climate.

The other is the story of the barrel itself, and the majority of those barrels around the world are the 53-gallon (200-liter) American Standard Barrel (ASB). Another large chunk of the rest are hogsheads, a 66-gallon (250-liter) cask almost invariably fashioned from recycled American barrel staves.

American barrels dominate the world of whiskey because the major types of American whiskey, like bourbon, must be matured in new oak barrels. Once that barrel is dumped, it cannot be used to make more bourbon. The American industry can recycle some of these barrels back into other products (Early Times, Mellow Corn, and an increasing number of American single malts, for example), but for the most part they want to sell those used barrels. Scotland, Ireland, Japan, and much of the rest of world whiskey use a production process that needs used barrels for maturation. The one industry feeds the others.

Although I've both heard and read of Europeans making the claim that the ASB is just an evolution of the hogshead, the record disproves that assertion. The ASB evolved hand in glove with the American whiskey industry, and is a product of experimentation, accident, and the need to meet changing demands. The ASB didn't reach its familiar 53-gallon form until the mid-20th century.

Two events in Thomas Jefferson's presidency started the process towards a handy, standardized American barrel into motion: the end of Alexander Hamilton's detested whiskey tax and the Louisiana Purchase.

According to Chris Morris, master distiller at Woodsford Reserve, "Kentuckians had access to the Ohio and Mississippi Rivers and no financial penalty for storing whiskey in barrels for long periods of time. So, now barrels began to be moved, and guess what, the bowed shape of today's ASB was the best for rolling and turning corners."

American coopers began adapting to the competing demands of volume, cost, and mobility. The next factor was the discovery of how air circulation improves maturation, which led Frederick Stitzel of Stitzel-Weller fame to patent the rickhouse design for whiskey warehousing in 1879. As it turns out, barrels need to be roughly the size of the modern ASB to make a rickhouse function according to design. Too big and the barrels are not only too difficult to handle, but also heavy enough to reduce the maximum height of the warehouse. Smaller barrels would cost warehouses storage efficiency.

The barrel that emerged over time, however, was the 48-gallon barrel. That was the American standard until the pressures of the Second World War forced further adaptation. With wood in short supply, distillers and coopers nudged the size up to make better use of rationed wood. They could not take this too far, however, since the barrel needed to fit into existing rickhouse infrastructure. Thus the 53-gallon ASB was born and has been with us ever since.

But who knows? White oak supply is a serious concern for the bourbon industry, and consequently the world whiskey industry as a whole (to say nothing of other users of ASBs, such as Tabasco hot sauce). This has mostly been centered around short-term concerns in logging and milling, but climate change is a more serious and longer term problem. Perhaps some new pressure will cause the industry to take another look at the ASB, and it will change yet again.

HOW A SCOTSMAN HELPED
INVENT KENTUCKY BOURBON

Dr. James Crow is the original Scotland-to-Kentucky, Scotch-to-bourbon connection. Born in Inverness in 1789, he graduated from Edinburgh University with degrees in chemistry and medicine in 1822. Crow immigrated to the United States directly thereafter and was in the Bluegrass by 1823.

At this juncture, another historic name in the history of Kentucky bourbon, Oscar Pepper, a second-generation whiskey distiller in Woodford County enters the picture. The exact date is uncertain, but sometime in the 1830s, Pepper hired Crow and made him his master distiller (it is possible Crow was hired on and then made master distiller later). It proved to be arguably the best hiring decision ever made in the bourbon industry.

Crow brought his Scots temperament and Edinburgh scientific training to the bourbon industry, codifying and perfecting techniques he found already in use in Kentucky. In particular, he is credited with turning the sour mash method of whiskey making into what we know today. Briefly, sour mash uses a starter of grain from previous fermentation batches to control bacterial spoilage of the mash, in much the same way that a starter is used in sourdough bread. In an era when germ theory was not fully developed and food-safe standards of sanitation were difficult to achieve, sour mash became a valuable industrial technique. Sour mashing also promoted consistent fermentation.

Sour mash was not a new idea. What Crow brought was litmus paper and a saccharimeter, applying laboratory rigor to the process and eliminating the guesswork. Crow also experimented with fermentation periods and distillation strength, which we know because he was said to extract less alcohol per bushel of grain than many of his peers. The Old Pepper Distillery, as it came to be called, also came equipped with a column still. This technology had only been patented in 1830, so it was quite the innovation at the time. Relying on Crow's perfection of bourbon-making techniques, Old Pepper introduced Old Crow bourbon, which became famous for its quality in antebellum America.

Dr. James Crow passed away in 1856. The Old Pepper Distillery has since evolved into Woodford Reserve.

This story can be found in many books about bourbon, but in my mind the most interesting part about the Dr. Crow story is untold and requires us to connect some dots. Crow left Scotland in 1823. That is the same year as the Excise Act that effectively legalized whisky making in Scotland. So, it can be said that at the same time the foundations were being laid for the Scotch industry as we recognize it today, a Scotsman was over in Kentucky drawing up the production details for what would become the Kentucky bourbon industry.

BONDED

"**B**ottled-in-bond" is at the same time a relic of a bygone era and a signpost of where American whiskey is today—and where it's headed in the near future. But to your typical consumer, seeing that on a label means the same thing it has for more than a century: this bottle contains quality whiskey.

The Bottled-in-Bond Act of 1897 is widely thought of as the first consumer protection act in US history, and as such was a trailblazer of the food and drug purity movement (think Upton Sinclair's *The Jungle*, which was published in 1906). Yet unlike much of the legislation that sprang from that reform movement, bottled-in-bond was actually the creation of big whiskey makers, who faced stiff competition from the period's rectification industry.

Rectifiers started out as *negociants*, or spirits traders. The term has become a dirty word among American whiskey history buffs, but not all rectifiers were disreputable. George Garvin Brown started out in this way in 1870, buying bourbon from other distillers and blending it together to make the original version of Old Forester. Across the Atlantic, most of the major brands of blended Scotch whisky, like Dewar's and Johnnie Walker, were created during the late nineteenth century in similar fashion.

The problem was that many in the American rectification industry weren't as scrupulous as Brown about producing a quality product. A common practice was to cut whiskey with neutral spirits (vodka, basically) or add burnt sugar, fruit juice, and/or tea for flavor and color. My favorite story about rectifier whiskey is the infamous tale that some especially noxious stuff was moonshine plus tobacco spit. This rotgut was competing with more expensively produced, proper bourbon, and the folks making that bourbon were not happy about it. Led by figures like James E. Pepper and E. H. Taylor, the Bottled-in-Bond Act was not just passed, but worded in such a way that it clearly favored distillers over nondistiller producers (NDPs).

The bonded stamp on the bottle guaranteed quality because the whiskey inside it was:

1. The product of a single distillery
2. Made in a single distilling season
3. At least four years old
4. Bottled at 100 proof, with only water added
   to adjust the proof

Yet what was important in 1900 became much less so in later times. As the bourbon industry entered the modern era, its premium brands were often standing well above the bonded standard. Knob Creek, a seminal bourbon for the small batch era of the 1990s, is typical: the whiskey comes entirely from Jim Beam, is bottled at 100 proof, but is at least nine years old.

Where bonded whiskey has found a new lease on life is on the labels of craft whiskey makers and new medium-sized distillers, such as New Riff. Craft whiskey has a reputation, earned in its early days, for being underaged. The familiar and traditional term "bottled-in-bond" guarantees a mature whiskey, and increasingly, many of these crafty bonded whiskeys are much older than the minimum four years.

THE ANGEL'S SHARE

No term in whiskey making is more poetic than "angel's share," so much so that it has gone on to enter the mainstream as the title of films, books, and songs. Conjuring as it does the image of a heavenly ghost sipping on spirits as it passes by the warehouse, it describes the steady evaporation of the whiskey as it matures in the barrel. The evaporation happens because, although the barrel is watertight, it isn't *vapor*-tight, because wood is a breathable material.

Angel's share is a phenomenon seen in whiskey industries around the world, although it takes a somewhat different shape depending on where the angels are doing their sipping. Kentucky, with its hot, humid summers and frosty winters, sees an evaporation rate averaging 5 percent per year. The milder climate of Scotland yields a rate of 2 percent, while the scorching temperatures of Texas produce up to 15 percent evaporation annually.

The climate not only drives how much whiskey evaporates, but also what, exactly, is evaporated. Andrea Wilson, the Master

of Maturation at Michter's Distillery, said, "When the barrel is in a very hot and dry environment, water molecules, which are smaller than alcohol molecules, are released and evaporate much faster and result in a higher alcohol concentration in the barrel." Likewise, "when the barrel is aging in cooler and more humid environments, water molecules find it harder to leave the barrel because they are pushing against water in the atmosphere so you end up with more alcohol leaving the barrel, which can cause a net decline in alcohol by volume."

Touching on the breathability of wood again, another factor influencing the angel's share is how the barrels are stored. The rickhouses of Kentucky were designed specifically to maximize air circulation around the barrels. Although that increases evaporation, it also improves on certain aspects of a bourbon's maturation in the bargain. On the opposite end of the spectrum, many of the distilleries in Scotland use a dunnage system, where the barrels are stacked on top of each other two or three rows high, on a gravel floor. This minimizes air flow around the barrels, helping them hang onto their contents.

A final variable in angel's share is the size of the barrel. In the United States, this was a constant until the twenty-first century, because the post–World War II bourbon industry relied almost exclusively on 53-gallon barrels. However, the craft spirits movement brought with it some larger barrels adapted from the wine industry, but many more smaller barrels. The smaller the barrel, the more evaporation it yields, so the 5- and 10-gallon barrels frequently used by early craft distillers saw steep losses to the angels.

Those tiny barrels are rare in Scotland, Ireland, and Japan. By and large, those industries prefer to go bigger. When they aren't relying on a used American 53-gallon standard barrel, they might rebuild them into 66-gallon hogsheads. Those countries also favor using huge casks from the Port, sherry, and Madeira wine industries, holding upwards of 132 gallons. One could say the angels find collecting their spirits tax from these huge barrels intimidating, because evaporation from them is substantially slower.

IT ISN'T JUST ANGELS WHO LIKE GOOD WHISKY

Shinto, or "the way of the gods," is Japan's indigenous religion, and is polytheistic and animistic in nature. Briefly, followers believe spirits inhabit the land, seasons, and other features of nature, and worship the spirits at a mixture of household, family, and public shrines. Japan is dotted with over 100,000 of the latter, some of which are entwined with the culture—and sometimes the physical establishment—of Japan's whisky distilleries.

Adjacent to Yamazaki is the venerable Shiio Shrine, whose foundation dates to the eighth century. The current gate for the shrine used to lie at the other end of the street but was moved to give trucks easier access to the distillery grounds. In its original location, distillery workers passed under it every day, making its present location a noteworthy bit of symbolism because the shrine is closely associated with the distillery nowadays. Recall that the Japanese word for gate is *torii*, same as the last name of the founder of Yamazaki's parent company, Suntory. Every year on November 11, starting at 11:11 a.m., the shrine holds an autumnal prayer ceremony for Shinjiro Torii.

Shinto features and rituals are commonplace at Japanese distilleries, so much so that it would be strange to not see Shinto garlands, the *shimenawa*, crowning the necks of Japanese pot stills. At Yoichi Distillery, a *shimenawa* also marks the doors for the distillery's first warehouse, marking the spot as sacred. After the conclusion of the New Year's holidays, a Shinto priest comes to Yoichi to bless the stills.

At Mars Whisky's Shinshu Distillery, there is a small shrine to the water god Mizugami on the grounds. Every morning, a prayer is held there before the workday begins, asking for a safe day and to make good whisky. After all, a distiller needs good water as a cornerstone for making whisky. Opened in 2016, Akkeshi Distillery made sure to install a small shrine directly above the spirit safe.

Japan, as a whole, is permeated with Shinto installations and rituals, so much so that Shinto is frequently incorporated into the practice of other religions in Japan. Although the two have mutually exclusive belief systems, it isn't unusual to see Japanese Christians practicing some Shintoism as a "perspective on life," while Buddhism and Shintoism are frequently practiced together. Keeping all that in mind, it should not be surprising that when the Japanese imported and adapted

Scotland's methods of making whisky, Shinto was just part and parcel of making it their own.

THE KING

The story behind Jack Daniel's is a two-parter, and the second half has little to do with Jack Daniel the man. Rather, it is about the modern version of the whiskey, a story that stands alone perfectly well and is wholly worth the telling. The central figure in this second half is Lem Motlow, Daniel's nephew, who took over the company at the end of 1907.

Motlow took the reins just in time to see his whiskey business driven from the Volunteer State. The temperance movement that would give rise to national Prohibition was especially strong in the South, and Tennessee went dry in 1909. Jack Daniel's the whiskey brand continued, initially relying on whiskey made in Alabama by his brother Frank "Spoon" Motlow. But Alabama soon went dry, too, whereupon sourcing was moved to St. Louis, Missouri. According to Nelson Eddy, the brand historian for Jack Daniel's, the reason Motlow looked to St. Louis was he had business ties there going back to Jack Daniel's gold medal–winning appearance at the 1904 World's Fair. Finally, 1919 brought the 18th Amendment and national Prohibition, and Lem Motlow was almost out of the whiskey business.

Almost, because Motlow sold some of his stocks of whiskey to Schenley Products, a company that held a rare medicinal whiskey license. He is also alleged to have tried to sell some stocks to George Remus, the so-called King of the Bootleggers.

Many distillers and brewers got out of the liquor business altogether during Prohibition, because when had an amendment to the Constitution ever been undone? The answer in the 1920s was never, and the answer to this day is just once: the repeal of Prohibition. Motlow was arguably the most determined of all to get back into it. He became active in politics in 1908, and in the following decades he would serve in the Tennessee House of Representatives and Senate, ceaselessly working towards any rollback of Tennessee's liquor laws that he could manage. It was a necessary campaign, because Tennessee did not repeal its statewide Prohibition until 1937, four years after the repeal of federal Prohibition. After that, Motlow

still had to secure permission to distill from Moore County. Only then could production restart at Jack Daniel's.

It's often joked that Jack Daniel's, the world's second largest whiskey brand, is made in a dry county. Except on a tour of the distillery, you can't drink it in Moore County, and the only place you can buy a bottle is the distillery gift shop. "There's always been that tension at the local level," says Eddy, between the distillery and the "dries," and this despite the major role the distillery has long played as an employer in the area. The most ironic example of this countywide exercise in cognitive dissonance is Jess Gamble, who served as master distiller from 1964 to 1966. Gamble was one of those ardently religious dries, who evaluated the whiskey strictly through nosing.

Despite Motlow working for the day when he could resume the family whiskey business, he was only half-ready for it. He had been keeping his ownership of the brand name alive by using "Jack Daniel's" for other business ventures, and the Motlow sawmill continued to operate on the distillery property. Jack Daniel's office, a little white clapboard house in the center of the modern property, was rented out to a family. Best of all, Motlow's other business interests meant he could self-finance the revival of the distillery. But many buildings were derelict, and the descriptions remind me of what I found at Old Taylor when I did urban exploring there (trees growing up through the roof, etc.). The first modern production run of Jack Daniel's whiskey had to wait until November 15, 1938.

Motlow insisted on reviving the classic brand, as it had existed, which meant he had to wait until he had properly mature whiskey before he could sell it as Jack Daniel's. In the interim, he sold a one-year-old whiskey called "Lem Motlow's Tennessee Sour Mash Whiskey." It's a move familiar to us today, when half the craft distillery start-ups sell gin or legal moonshine while working on their in-house whiskey, but with the added wrinkle that Motlow was preserving the Jack Daniel's name for the good stuff. His name went on the stopgap whiskey. Coming from a proud man with a reputation for irritability, that move shows just how highly Motlow prized the Daniel's name. Lem Motlow's namesake brand persisted as a curiosity until 1992.

Mirroring how Lem Motlow took over Jack Daniel's whiskey just before it was chased out of Tennessee, he was able to revive it just as his health began to fail. Motlow suffered a stroke in 1941, was wheelchair-bound thereafter, and died of a cerebral hemorrhage in 1947. The distillery passed to his four sons, Reagor, Robert, Daniel, and Connor. The brothers, especially the eldest Reagor, guided the distillery from revival into national popularity, but by the mid-1950s they had hit a double wall.

Jack Daniel's had become a victim of its own success, in that demand had outpaced supply. The company needed to expand, but the Motlow family did not have the financial resources necessary to undertake both the capital investment and to pay the excise taxes that such a major expansion of output would entail. But Nelson Eddy thinks another problem confronting the future of the company was just as important: none of the Motlow brothers had a son. This was the 1950s, the South, and the unseemly liquor trade, so the idea of passing the family business onto one of the Motlow women was out of the question. The Motlows went looking for a buyer.

They were committed to the family's classic Jack Daniel's production method and continuing in that fashion was a nonnegotiable point. One suitor was Schenley Industries, but the Motlow brothers weren't interested. Their father's past dealings with Schenley probably colored the brothers' opinions, but in a larger sense, I doubt they believed they could trust either Schenley boss Lewis Rosenstiel or a publicly traded corporation in general to keep any promises to make Jack Daniel's in the traditional way for the long term. Another suitor was Brown-Forman. Although also a publicly traded company, it was majority owned by the Brown family (and still is today). Schenley offered more money, but the Motlows chose Brown-Forman.

Reagor Motlow continued as the company president until 1963 and served on Brown-Forman's board of directors for some time thereafter. The Motlows faded out of the Jack Daniel's story, but not from Lynchburg and thereabouts. The family is still the largest landowner in Moore County, with roads and the local community college named after them.

The time when anyone at Brown-Forman might have considered getting around their agreement and changing things at Jack Daniel's has long since passed. As the biggest brand in American whiskey, it is the crown jewel in their empire. Things have grown quite a lot down there in Lynchburg: the 99 bushels of corn a day that Jack Daniel set as his personal production ceiling is now 95 *acres* worth per day. But many elements remain that would have been recognizable to a visitor in the 1950s, and how the whiskey is made has changed only in scale (vastly in scale, but the particulars remain fixed).

One clear illustration of the sheer size of the operation is that Jack Daniel's has its own fire department. I long believed that that factoid meant they sponsored the county fire service, but no, it is a separate volunteer fire company, staffed by employees and paid for by the company. Specializing in putting out alcohol fires, the JD fire brigade has stocks of fire-extinguishing foam outstripping those found at any airport east of the Mississippi. The 1996 disaster suffered by Heaven Hill in particular prompted Jack Daniel's to raise the bar on their fire readiness.

The culture clash between distillery and dries in Moore County continues, and this despite the tide of temperance in Tennessee (and Kentucky) receding and how Jack Daniel's has evolved into a third- and even fourth-generation employer for many of the county's families. Talk of whiskey dynasties most often focuses on the role of the master distiller, owner, or director, but it is dynastic talk of a different scale to say the majority of the workers at Jack Daniel's are legacies.

Among many others, Nelson Eddy appreciates the grudging tolerance or continuing friction with the dries, and the singular virtue of making whiskey in a dry county. Outside of Jack Daniel's, Moore County is still very rural, with Lynchburg at its center, a town complete with a working 19th century courthouse. The outsized shadow of the distillery would very likely drown the remaining authenticity of that charming county seat with bars were it to go wet. Looking through that lens, one can get a little insight into what the temperance movement was all about.

THE LINCOLN COUNTY PROCESS

Whether Tennessee whiskey is bourbon is probably *the* classic bar debate about booze, and like all such debates, it is argued more from emotion than fact. I've found those most passionate in indulging in it are strongly attached to their Kentucky bourbon (either the Kentucky or the bourbon part, sometimes both), and paradoxically that attachment is a path that leads to *both* arguments. Being a certain stripe of bourbon snob leads one in the direction of dismissing Tennessee whiskey's distinctiveness by declaring that either it is just another bourbon or that it isn't worthy of being called bourbon, merely whiskey from Tennessee. The most fun is had when one of these folks runs across a solid fan of Jack Daniel's, who will advocate that Tennessee whiskey isn't bourbon because it is so distinctive and wonderful.

My take is that the argument was settled in 2013, when the State of Tennessee passed its whiskey law, formally defining just what Tennessee whiskey is. The description makes it quite clear that Tennessee whiskey is bourbon plus one significant step in production, and that step is the Lincoln County Process (LCP).

The LCP is the original old-school shortcut for time spent in the barrel. The power of charcoal to remove impurities was known to some early American distillers, just as it was to European distillers. Other people, including slaves abducted from Africa, would have known about charcoal's qualities through water filtration. Before the end of the Second World War, the practice was referred to by distillers as charcoal leaching and is still widely referred to as charcoal mellowing. Filtering the new make whiskey through hardwood charcoal removes ("leaches") some of the trace volatile chemicals in the spirit that contribute to the harshness of new make whiskey, mellowing the product a little before maturation mellows it further.

The reason I like to think of the LCP as the first working shortcut on maturation is that when you compare whiskeys made with the method against their peers made in Kentucky (say Jack Daniel's versus Jim Beam or Evan Williams), what you find is that the charcoal mellowed whiskey has achieved a comparable level of smoothness two to three years ahead of the Kentucky schedule. Not flavor or complexity, per se, but definitely smoothness. The charcoal filtration is an added cost to making whiskey, sure, but the maker could wind up getting that back by saving on a few years of paying the angel's share, saving on the overhead from barrel storage, and so forth.

The biggest misconception about charcoal filtration is that it puts a maple flavor into the whiskey, so much so that some reviewers seem to go out of their way to find maple notes in everything made with the LCP. Once I asked Chris Fletcher, the current master distiller at Jack Daniel's, why sugar maple was chosen, and he told me it was just because sugar maple is a widely available hardwood in Tennessee, but it isn't used for much else. Although Tennessee's sugar maples can make maple syrup, that isn't done very much anywhere in the South. Overall, it makes sense once you know that white oak is needed for things like making barrels, hickory for smoking, and other hardwoods like walnut are prized for making furniture. Moreover, the filtration is about taking things out of the whiskey, not putting them in.

Beyond the stipulation that the filtration take place before entering the barrel, there are no further guidelines on how the LCP is to be carried out, and methods vary. Jack Daniel's is famous for its "Extra Blessing," which is what they call it when they slowly drip new make into a vat with ten feet of charcoal in it. George Dickel chills their new make before passing it through the charcoal, while Nelson's Greenbrier simply fills their old barrels with charcoal, drills a hole in the bottom, and filters their whiskey that way.

OVERLOOKED STORIES OF AFRICAN AMERICANS IN WHISKEY

The story of Nathan Green is remarkable for just how long it languished in obscurity. The life of "Uncle Nearest," as he was known to family and friends, is the untold chapter in the foundation of Jack Daniel's, the avatar of the roles enslaved and then freed African American people played in America's early whiskey industry, and the beginning of a movement that today is gaining increasing momentum: African Americans claiming some ownership of the whiskey business.

Green was a slave, owned by a labor company and hired out to Dan Call, the Tennessee preacher, grocer, farmer, and distiller who has long been noted in the legend of Jack Daniel's as the man who gave Jasper "Jack" Daniel a job in the 1850s, when Daniel was just a boy. Daniel did odd jobs around the Call property, but was particularly drawn to Call's whiskey-making operation, so that is where he ultimately came to work. Green was the skilled distiller who oversaw that operation, despite being only a little older than Daniel, and it was Green rather than Call who taught Daniel how to make the whiskey that would eventually become Jack Daniel's Old No. 7. Green was freed during the Civil War, and continued to work at the still—first for Call, and then Daniel.

The seminal role that Green played in Jack Daniel's training as a whiskey maker has never been secret, as Daniel is known to have praised Green as the man who taught him about making whiskey, and he employed not just Nathan, but also three of his sons. Green's role as one of Daniel's mentors appeared in print in a book, *Jack Daniel's Legacy*, published in 1967. Moreover, Green's descendants have counted among the numerous generational employees at Jack Daniel's, a legacy that continues to this day. Down in Moore County, the story has long been part of the local folklore. So instead of being a secret, the Nathan "Nearest" Green story was simply ignored by the wider world until it began appearing in the media in 2016 and 2017.

And Green was hardly the only slave working as a distiller in the antebellum Upper South. Indeed, the role of enslaved people in the whiskey industry is known to predate there being a state of Tennessee. George Washington's Mount Vernon distillery was one of the largest whiskey-making operations in the country at the end of the 18th century. The development of the modern, living history distillery project at Mount Vernon overlapped with greater attention being given to the history of its enslaved community. Slaves named Daniel, Hanson, James, Nat, Peter, and Timothy ran that distillery for Washington, and on top of their contributions were those of the enslaved coopers who made barrels on the estate.

The role African Americans played in early whiskey making extends to Kentucky as well. During her time at Kentucky State University, Dr. Erin Wiggins Gilliam was particularly engaged in academic research into enslaved people working for distilling operations in Kentucky. In one example, working with a local western Kentucky historian named Gary Gardner, Gilliam discovered documents that told the story of a slave worker leased out to distilleries around Hodgenville. His owner's records reveal that this worker cost substantially more than the wages of a white day laborer of the time, strongly suggesting that he was, like Green, a skilled distillery man.

As further research is done on the subject, more parallels with Green's life have come into view. A common theme throughout the whiskey business is how it is so often a family trade, and that was just as true for its emancipated workers as it has been for anyone else. In 2022, I was privileged to hear a lecture on a neighborhood in late 19th century Frankfort, Kentucky, that was mostly populated by the families of African American distillery workers. Stories like that one put a link in a chain that goes back to the early and middle 1800s, the pre-Emancipation era.

What makes modern times different is how these stories have been lifted up and intertwined into African Americans taking ownership of their place in American whiskey making, both figuratively and literally. In 2017, entrepreneur Fawn Weaver launched the Uncle Nearest whiskey brand, and that company is in the midst of erecting a distillery on a still-working Tennessee walking horse farm on the outskirts of Shelbyville. Their master distiller is Victoria Eady Butler, a descendant of Green and the first African American woman known to hold that title. In her work as blender/taster for the currently sourced line of Uncle Nearest whiskeys, she has twice won the Master Blender of the Year award from *Whisky Magazine*, among other accolades.

Following hard on the heels of Weaver's launch of Uncle Nearest, two black-owned companies began staking claims in Kentucky bourbon: Louisville's Brough Brothers and Lexington's Fresh Bourbon. Sean and Tia Edwards registered their company, Fresh Bourbon, in 2017 and have been contract producing their whiskey through Hartfield & Co. in Paris, Kentucky. Contract production is an important distinction, since it means a company is having their spirits made according to their own recipe, as opposed to simply sourcing it from already existing stockpiles. As Joe Magliocco, president of Michter's, described it, contract producing is "doing your own cooking in someone else's kitchen." Fresh Bourbon launched their product in 2020, during the COVID-19 pandemic.

Over in Louisville, Victor, Christian, and Bryson Yarborough acquired their West End property in 2018, released sourced bourbon in 2019, and opened production at their West End distillery in 2021. Both Fresh Bourbon and Borough Brothers claim to be the first African American company to make bourbon in Kentucky. It's a hair-splitting argument familiar to anyone who knows America's craft whiskey scene, which is replete with competing claims to be the first distillery to make this spirit in that location. The Yarboroughs' claim is built on being first to open their own distillery, while the Edwards point to having the first registered company, their much earlier contract production, and getting a whiskey on the market first. Throw the Louisville-Lexington rivalry into the mix, and I'm sure this dispute will become the grist of more than a few bar debates in central Kentucky in the years to come.

Regardless of who one actually judges to have been first, the arrival of these two companies in the Bluegrass State is most welcome. Heretofore, the face of African Americans in bourbon has been Freddie Johnson, a third-generation employee at Buffalo Trace and their VIP Visitor Lead (i.e., chief tour guide). Although Johnson is a popular, well-known, and highly esteemed figure (he was elected to the Kentucky Bourbon Hall of Fame in 2018), as well as part of his own family trade legacy, it's well past time for some people of color who are making bourbon in their own right to join him on that stage.

In much the same way that whiskey making has spread nationwide due to the craft boom, so it has also been joined by African American distillers outside of the Upper South. Black-owned whiskey companies around the United States include:

- 18th Street Distillery (Hammond, Indiana)
- Du Nord Craft Spirits (Minneapolis, Minnesota)
- Gravesend-Braxton Distillers (Wyandanch, New York)
- Guidance Whiskey (Nashville, Tennessee)
- Highway Distillery (Houston, Texas)
- Painted Stave Distilling (Smyrna, Delaware)

WHISKEY IN THE AMERICAN CIVIL WAR

In 1863, a story began making the rounds in American newspapers. Well, Yankee newspapers. When confronted with criticism that General Grant was prone to taking his whiskey and going on a bender, Lincoln replied, "Tell me what brand it is, and I'll send a barrel to each of the other generals."

That brand is supposed to have been Old Crow, which Grant is known to have favored, at least later on during his presidency. My favorite Civil War whiskey story has nothing to do with generals, though, because it is better rooted in the period's whiskey business and its wartime reality. Today, the name W.L. Weller is recognized as a brand of wheated bourbon from Buffalo Trace. That is because the man, William Larue Weller, is one of a handful of people reputed to have invented wheated bourbon, and in the 1860s Weller was running a family bourbon business out of Louisville.

In a very Kentucky kind of story, two of Weller's brothers went South. John Weller served in the Orphan Brigade, the Confederate infantry unit raised from Kentuckians. He became a captain and was wounded at Chickamauga. But another brother, Charles Weller, stayed with William to run the family business, which is the larger story of Kentucky during the war: wherever a Kentuck's heart may have been leaning, his pocketbook was inevitably nailed to the North.

Charles didn't escape the war, though. In 1862, he rode to Nashville to collect on a business debt. With the outbreak of war that kind of travel was quite hazardous as rural Tennessee and Kentucky descended into lawlessness. Charles Weller was murdered by bandits on the road.

In the popular imagination, all those Johnnie Rebs and Billy Yanks were draining cups of bourbon, some form of proto–Jack Daniel's or Pennsylvania rye. These notions of what those whiskeys actually were are mostly erroneous. For one thing, the Confederate States of America enacted Prohibition in 1862 as a war conservation measure, to direct grain and copper away from making alcohol and to the war effort. Civil War era Prohibition was even less effective than the nationwide effort that followed six decades later, but it nonetheless put a dent in things. Whiskey making in the South went on, but it largely took the form of backwoods moonshining. Where Jack Daniel and Nearest Green were making whiskey for the Reverend Call during the war, for example, is a distinctly out of sight place even today.

In the North, however, the whiskey industry was embraced as a way to fuel the Union war machine. Federal excise taxes had been retired in 1817, after being reintroduced during the War of 1812. Lincoln enacted a "sin tax" on whiskey of 20 cents on the proof gallon in 1862, and by 1865 it was $1.50 per gallon. That $1.50 is approximately what your typical blacksmith in the North earned for a day's work; a Union private was paid $16 a month in 1865.

Most of that whiskey wasn't made in Kentucky, however, nor Maryland or Pennsylvania, and it certainly wasn't captured on a raid into Tennessee or Virginia. A lot of it came from Grant's home state of Illinois, where Peoria was growing into the alcohol capital of the United States. The tax records prove it: half of all the sin tax collected during the war came from the Peoria-Pekin Fifth Federal Tax District. It was the beginning of an industrial alcohol boom in Peoria, which would lead it to becoming home to some of the largest whiskey distilleries in the country by the time of Prohibition.

WHY IT'S OLD NO. 7 IN A SQUARE BOTTLE

The very look of Jack Daniel's has taken on a life of its own. It's iconic, and Brown-Forman is well known for taking anyone who so much as skirts the look of a bottle of JD Old No. 7 to court. That look and label have become the font of a clutch of stories, some intertwined with the man Jack Daniel and some with his whiskey.

The company began bottling its own whiskey in 1895 (this was a quarter century after George Garvin Brown, founder of parent company Brown-Forman, made Old Forester the first bourbon sold bottled by its maker, rather than the retailer). There are examples of rounded clear glass jugs and bottles that predate the now familiar rigidly defined, squared bottle styling, and there are two official explanations as to why the bottle is squared. The practical version is the squared shape was chosen because it was more stable in the packing and shipping of the day. The colorful version is that it was the last design shown to Daniel, who chose it saying, "A square bottle for a square shooter." My personal favorite is very much unofficial: "It's square so it don't roll off the passenger's seat while you're driving."

I sometimes wish there were *only* seven theories as to how the core Jack Daniel's whiskey came to be called "Old No. 7." The consensus story among the experts, including *Blood and Whiskey* author Peter Krass, is that Daniel was incensed when the state of Tennessee changed his distillery registration number from 7 to 16 in a tax district reorganization. Worse, his was the only number so changed. That registration number was required to be on the label, so he emblazoned it with "Old No. 7" to head off any confusion.

The official historian, Nelson Eddy, is dubious about that explanation. "He had his name on these things, so why use the number seven to promote it?"

Eddy also dismissed the explanation that Daniel was a short king and a ladies man, and the code refers to his seven girlfriends . . . but says if it were true, it would explain why he never married.

Another explanation I heard is that Jack Daniel named it No. 7 because he started branding it as such in 1887, had to put something on there, and took that last number of the year. It's also been said he tried several mash recipes, but the seventh one turned out to be the one chosen. Or that seven was inside the barrel head on a honey barrel he shipped to a client, who then asked for more of that number seven. Similar is the tale of seven barrels being shipped down to Tullahoma, reported lost, and then found again with the replacements en route, so the originals were marked "Old No. 7." The one I firmly discount is that the brand was named after seven barrels that were sent to the 1904 World's Fair in St. Louis, which obviously isn't true because it was already being called Old No. 7 by then. The simplest is it's named for the lucky number seven.

This bit of brand identity has no official explanation, but the one I find most interesting is the one that comes from within the family. The Motlows were known to tell people that Jack used to have a friend and customer who owned seven pharmacies, and at the time he thought that owning that many pharmacies was the pinnacle of success.

Regardless, we'll never know for sure why the bottle and the labeling were chosen. That is why these physical features make for such good bar stories and debates to this day. After all, you can see them in just about every bar on the planet.

JASPER DANIEL THE MAN, JACK DANIEL THE MYTH

Jack Daniel is both a brand and a man, and plenty of myths have grown up around both of them. For example, it is an open question just when Jasper Newton Daniel (his real, full name) was even born, with references spanning from 1848 to 1850. When I was talking about this discrepancy with Nelson Eddy, he raised the possibility that Daniel himself was part of fudging his age before dismissing it.

"Who shaves just two years off their age like that?" he asked. I countered he might have been overly sensitive about turning 40 or 50. Many people are. It sounds like the kind of thing that a man with more than a little vanity might do, and then keep on telling the fib ever after. Certainly, there must be more to the conflicting dates than faulty recordkeeping.

I have also heard it said that Daniel was de facto chased out of the family home by his stepmother, after the death of his father. Daniel's own mother died shortly after he was born, so he never knew her. The family had modest means, the new stepmother was saddled with several children, and the trope of the evil stepmother has never sat right with me. What the timeline shows is that Daniel was already working for Dan Call, the man who would eventually employ him in the distilling business, before his father died. We know Jack didn't get along with his stepmother, but it is unlikely he was chased or hounded out of the house, and Jack helped care for his stepsiblings following his departure.

But the story that has always given me the most trouble is that Jack Daniel couldn't open his safe one day, gave the thing a swift kick that broke his toe, the toe became infected, and it killed him. Even assuming that you heard the same version of the story that I did, which is that he died after his gangrenous foot was amputated, it felt like something was missing (besides his foot). I'm a history geek, and I know perfectly well that while people died from infections all the time before the invention of sulfa drugs and antibiotics in the mid-20th century, I also know the success rate for amputations of the feet and hands during the Civil War, which was surprisingly high.

But nonetheless, Daniel later had to have his leg amputated. In what must have been a miserable stretch of several months, he endured repeat surgeries and then died.

A modern theory is that Daniel was diabetic. He was an older, rotund man on a Southern diet who liked a good drink, and these days we know that diabetes should be following right behind a fellow of that description. The notion that perhaps diabetes compounded Daniel's recovery from surgery is a logical one. Yet some have taken this a step further and given the tale a modern twist. It had already been asserted long ago that kicking the safe had nothing to do with his demise, and Daniel contracted the infection in some other way. Now it has been theorized that it was never an infection at all, and that diabetes took Daniel's foot and then leg. It's the internet age, diabetes claiming feet and legs is a fixture of modern life, and new stories spread rapidly.

Kicking the safe is the official version, and historian Nelson Eddy's opinion is that Daniel was done in, like James A.

Garfield, by too much inept medical attention. Daniel was already in failing health, and the painful treatments and operations were too much for him. As for the idea that it was never kicking the safe or Daniel's death wasn't even connected to infection, Eddy maintains the safe and the gangrene are how the story has always been told, since before the day Daniel died.

LEM MOTLOW, MURDERER

Jack Daniel's is home to some of whiskey's tallest and most charming tales, but also one of its most sordid. In 1923, Lem Motlow shot a man to death and got away with it.

Motlow was indicted for his part in the bootlegging case involving George Remus and a store of Jack Daniel's whiskey in St. Louis, Missouri. After making a brief court appearance on March 17, 1924, followed by dinner and drinks with friends, Motlow boarded the overnight train for the journey to Nashville and onto home. The sleeping car porter, Ed Wallis, asked Motlow for his ticket, but he could not find it. Motlow, who was thought to have had too much to drink, became angry at being challenged by Wallis, who was black. The conductor, Clarence Pullis (a white man), intervened in the argument, which allegedly had already turned violent. Motlow drew his pistol and fired it twice, hitting Pullis once in the belly. All of this transpired before the train had even left St. Louis.

Pullis died of his wound, and Motlow was charged with murder. A man of some means with connections in St. Louis dating back to the 1904 World's Fair, Motlow assembled a crack legal team for his defense. Among his character witnesses was Tennessee's governor, Austin Peay. Despite the victim being white, the defense was based squarely on playing the race card.

When Wallis testified, defense lawyers mocked his accent and asked him if belonged to any civil rights groups. During his own testimony, Motlow accused Wallis of attacking him, grabbing him by the throat.

The defense's closing argument was littered with racial slurs, spoke of Wallis not knowing his place, and continued to allege that he was a civil rights activist, all in an effort to inflame the jury. The defense's tactics were about attacking the credibility of the sole witness and proving self-defense while also aiming to shift the focus of the trial from the murder of a working-class white man onto a supposed uppity black man laying his hands on a prominent white businessman and politician. In a verdict typical of the Jim Crow era, an all-white St. Louis jury found Motlow not guilty. The foreman, Frederick Smith, was quoted as saying "We didn't believe the negro." Many jurors came around to shake Motlow's hand after the trial.

Motlow went back to St. Louis later to stand trial a second time, this time for the bootlegging case. He was found not guilty on that charge, as well. One would like to think that having been obviously guilty of manslaughter (if not murder) and bootlegging would have darkened the man's reputation, but he was elected to the Tennessee House of Representatives in 1933, and then the state senate in 1939. Motlow well and truly got away with all of it.

JACK AND COKE ARE BLOOD RELATIONS

Jack Daniel's and Coca-Cola is one of the world's classic cocktails. Although I know quite a few people prefer a different whiskey to mix with their soft drink of choice—one of my neighbors from my Washington, DC, days was adamant that Evan Williams and RC Cola was the way to go—none of these preferences have reached the level of bar staple. In my experience, the only mixer that surpasses Jack and Coke for ubiquity is the rum and Coke, and I say surpass because that one has its own name, the Cuba Libre.

Yet there is a little more to this standard than compatibility or that each is a leading brand from an adjacent region of the South. Jack Daniel's and Coca-Cola are, very loosely, family.

Lem Motlow's great-great-grandparents were Obediah Hooper and Massilva Marvula Brooks. Another descendant of that pair was Asa Griggs Candler. Born in 1851, Candler sat right between Daniel and Motlow (uncle and nephew) in terms of age and was the third cousin of Motlow. He bought a soft drink formula from a chemist named John Pemberton in 1888. A few years later, he founded a company around the production and sale of that soft drink and called it the Coca-Cola Company.

Neither Motlow nor Candler actually created the respective drinks they are associated with, and in Motlow's case he did not start the company either. There is no evidence the two men ever met, and therefore they probably did not. Yet neither Jack Daniel's nor Coca-Cola, two of the world's biggest drinks brands (albeit very different kinds of drinks), would exist today were it not for them. So, it could be said that Jack Daniel's and Coca-Cola really do belong together, because they share a little DNA. Underlining the relationship is that even with the abundance of ready-to-drink mixers of spirits and soft drinks available on store shelves (Jameson and Crown Royal both have one), the only one Coca-Cola is involved with is Jack Daniel's. A drinker too bothered or lazy to mix the pair themselves can get them in bottles and cans, using either classic Coke or Coke Zero.

REVENGE IS BEST SERVED COLD, WITH A POUR OF GEORGE DICKEL

For most of the late 20th century, there were just two whiskey distilleries in Tennessee: Jack Daniel's and Cascade Hollow (popularly known as George Dickel), and one of them was founded as an act of revenge on the other. If the Motlow family had sold Jack Daniel's to a different buyer, we wouldn't have George Dickel Tennessee Whiskey as we know it today.

As detailed earlier, the Motlow siblings sold the distillery to Brown-Forman in 1956. But they had more suitors than Brown-Forman, and chief among them was Lewis Rosenstiel, founder and longtime head of Schenley Industries. Back in the 1950s, Brown-Forman was just a midsized liquor company, while Schenley was one of the "Big Four" that dominated the industry. Worse, Rosenstiel was not a man to mildly accept a "no" while seeing the Motlows sell to a smaller rival. Dubbed "The Bad Boy of Bourbon" by Moonshine University, Rosenstiel was indicted for bootlegging, but never convicted. He was reputed to have mob connections, loved palling around with notorious shyster Roy Cohn, and was the sort of character people loved to hate. His fourth wife, Susan, claimed for decades that in 1958 she saw Rosenstiel, Cohn, and FBI director J. Edgar Hoover in an orgy with a couple of blonde young men. That story has been debunked, but it is indicative of the kind of venom Rosenstiel engendered.

One of the many brands owned by Schenley was Cascade Whiskey, which, before Tennessee's 1909 statewide Prohibition, had been made in Cascade Hollow. By the 1950s, it had morphed into George Dickel's Cascade Bourbon, and was being made in Frankfort, Kentucky, at the OFC Distillery (later George T. Stagg and now called Buffalo Trace). Dickel was a Nashville area businessman in the late 19th century, who at one point owned a majority stake in the Cascade Hollow distillery. In the same deal, Dickel gained exclusive rights to bottle and sell Cascade Whiskey.

In the wake of being spurned by the Motlows, Rosenstiel decided it was time to bring Cascade Whiskey home. Schenley rebuilt the distillery in 1958, and revived Cascade Whiskey using George Dickel's original records detailing the production process. However, Cascade Bourbon had been marketed as a cheap brand, and had a down-market reputation. Rather than rehabilitate the name, the decision was made to name the new whiskey George Dickel. The first bottles were shipped in 1964.

Thus, modern George Dickel was created specifically to compete with Jack Daniel's, out of spite rather than commercial ambition. However, by the time Schenley broke ground in Cascade Hollow, it was already too late. Jack Daniel's was Frank Sinatra's "nectar of the gods," which played a key role in popularizing the brand. The peak of Sinatra's fame overlapped neatly with that 1958 to 1964 window in which Dickel was being readied for market. By the time Dickel got onto store shelves, Jack was already well on its way to becoming a cultural icon.

SHE'S DONE BIG WHISKEY AND CRAFT WHISKEY

The last several years have seen a changing of the guard among the master distillers of the Kentucky and Tennessee Majors (i.e., the big distilleries). Only a few of the chief whiskey makers who were holding their respective tillers in the early 2010s are still holding them today—and those few have seemingly anointed their successors. So, the big makers of Kentucky bourbon and Tennessee whiskey have mostly newish faces running things, and among those new faces is one woman whose story illustrates how modern American whiskey is changing like never before: Nicole Austin.

Austin doesn't hail from a whiskey-making family nor was she born in the Upper South, and she did not undertake her education with an eye on breaking into the business. That said, she did follow a course that set her up well to pursue it later: she got her bachelor's degree in chemistry and engineering from Manhattan College in 2006 (a college in Riverdale, New York, and not on the namesake island). Whiskey first grabbed her attention when she was out on a date, thanks to a bartender who did what all the best bartenders do: sell drinks by telling drink tales.

Her interest in possibly changing her career path came at a good time, because, as she has put it before, "I didn't have the right last name to work in Kentucky or the right degree for Scotland." Austin was fortuitous to look at how to break into the whiskey business when she did, because she was doing it as the craft whiskey movement in America was just beginning to gain steam. If she had asked the question "How am I going to do this?" upon graduating college, she wouldn't have had many answers at all. As it turns out, when she did pose the question there was a start-up distillery over in the Navy Yard in Brooklyn: Kings County Distillery. She signed on as master blender in 2010.

Working in a small, new distillery meant an all-hands-on-deck experience common in start-ups, but as Austin describes it, working for Kings County in those days was a side hustle and more of a volunteer labor of love. She didn't leave behind her first career in environmental engineering until the late Dave Pickerell—ex-Maker's Mark master distiller who became a consultant and had a hand in starting so many brands and micro-distillery projects that he was dubbed "The Johnny Appleseed of Whiskey"—hired her in 2012. She worked for Pickerell for three years, finally doing whiskey full-time, before leaving his company to do some consulting on her own.

Austin was then hired on by her first big whisky company, William Grant & Sons, and sent to their shiny new Tullamore Dew distillery in Ireland. Clearly a rising star in the business at a time when the business was expanding rapidly, Diageo offered her the long vacant top slot at Cascade Hollow Distilling in Tennessee. Austin was just 33 years old. By way of comparison, her peer Chris Fletcher was almost 40 when he rose from heir apparent to master distiller at Jack Daniel's, despite being the grandson of a previous master distiller there.

Since taking over in 2018, Austin has raised the profile of the George Dickel brand, previously the sleeper of America's big legacy whiskey brands. Although none of the whiskey involved was made by her, Austin's blending skills are certainly on display in things like the George Dickel Bottled in Bond line.

Austin is still a young woman, with the bulk of her career in the future. But for now, she is one of very few people whose personal story has one foot in America's big distillery whiskey, one in craft whiskey, and a couple of toes wetted from her time across the Atlantic.

EZRA BROOKS STARTED AS A JACK DANIEL'S KNOCKOFF

George Dickel was not the only brand whose creation was inspired by the success of Jack Daniel's. Sales of Jack Daniel's were expanding dramatically even before their acquisition by Brown-Forman in 1956, and well before the years when identification with the Rat Pack cemented its place in pop culture. This led to a demand crunch by the late 1950s, forcing Brown-Forman to allocate its supply. The unsatisfied demand and gaps on shelves opened the door to imitators, the most famous of which is Ezra Brooks.

As documented in the civil suit *Jack Daniel's Distillery, Inc. v. Hoffman Distilling Co.*, circa 1960, Frank Hoffman set out to create a sourced Kentucky bourbon brand to filch away some of that Jack Daniel's thunder. His new brand, Ezra Brooks, wasn't merely inspired by Jack Daniel's—it was a blatant rip-off. As detailed in court documents, everything from the bottle to the color of the label to the text on that label was not even so much as a quarter-step removed from the presentation of Jack Daniel's. Hoffman even claimed (falsely) in his advertising that Ezra Brooks was in short supply, just like Jack Daniel's.

One problem confronting Hoffman was that Jack Daniel's used the Lincoln County Process, a key factor to the quality of what was in their bottles of Old No. 7 whiskey. There were no stocks of Kentucky bourbon lying around that had been filtered through hardwood charcoal prior to maturation in the barrel, so Hoffman's company filtered it through charcoal after the barrels were dumped, prior to bottling. It's a key distinction, but one that could be glossed over on the labels and in marketing.

Despite the flagrant poaching, the court found in favor of Hoffmann, ruling that the clearly different name of the brand and the fact that it originated in Kentucky, not Tennessee, provided sufficient distinction. It would not be the last time Jack Daniel's found itself in a difficult legal battle to protect its identity. As recently as 2023, the US Supreme Court ruled on a Jack Daniel's trademark dispute involving the dog toy "Bad Spaniels," spoofing Jack Daniel's. Brown-Forman won that case.

Ezra Brooks would continue to mislead the public about being in high demand and short supply well into the 1960s. The brand would change hands many times, eventually leaving behind its roots as a Jack Daniel's knockoff but continuing to employ charcoal filtration after barrel maturation. Today the brand is owned by Luxco, also owners of Lux Row Distillery in Bardstown, Kentucky. Luxco, in turn, is owned by MGP, the Indiana distillery that provides much of the aged whiskey stock relied upon by sourced brands around America.

Ezra Brooks wasn't the only Jack Daniel's imitator. Jim Beam introduced their own, Jim Beam Choice. This green-labeled, five-year-old version of Jim Beam was, like Ezra Brooks, charcoal filtered after maturation. The brand hung on as a bourbon curiosity for decades, but has since been discontinued.

THE BEAM DYNASTY

"Bourbon dynasties" are very much a thing in America. For many a bourbon enthusiast, the job title of master distiller as a hereditary position seems more natural than the job going to a newcomer, someone with no family connections and an unknown last name. However true that notion is in practice—and there are many bourbon families in Kentucky—the idea has as much to do with the Beams as with anybody. Certainly, no other family name is as synonymous with bourbon as Beam.

Like the best Kentucky stories (including my own family history), the Beam dynasty begins in the earliest days of the Union. Johannes Böhm was a German immigrant who moved to Kentucky in the 1780s. Excepting a few large producers like George Washington, most whiskey of that era was made by small farmer-distillers, and Böhm was fairly typical of this class. He would grow a large crop of corn, and whatever wasn't needed to feed the family or the livestock would be turned into whiskey. As an agricultural product destined for market, it's useful to think of whiskey as condensed grain that doesn't spoil. Böhm eventually had his name anglicized to Jacob Beam, but this may or may not have happened during his lifetime. Over the years, I've read and heard the story about what happened with that very German name told both ways.

In 1820, Jacob's son David took over what had grown from an agricultural side hustle to a prosperous business. For context, David assumed control from Jacob in the same decade that Dr. James Crow was busy turning bourbon making into a scientifically controlled process, and David played a major role in expanding the Beam bourbon business. His son, David M. Beam, took things a step further by moving the distillery to Nelson County in 1854, so it would be in easy reach of the newly opened Louisville & Nashville Railroad. The Beam family brand, Old Tub, was shipped by rail across the country. The seat of Nelson County, by the way, is Bardstown, nowadays referred to as the "Bourbon Capital of the World."

But the man who probably did more than anything to cement the family legacy was James Beauregard Beam, because he was the one who steered the family business through the difficult years of Prohibition. People in the World War I era liquor business lacked modern hindsight and did not know that the 18th Amendment and Prohibition would become America's greatest

failed experiment in social engineering. For many of that time, temperance was written into the Constitution, and most in the liquor business quite reasonably thought it was settled: the "dries" had won the argument. Whether it was brewing or spirits or winemaking, most thought their business was dead, so it was time to move on.

James B. Beam wasn't among the many who threw in the towel. Much like his peer in Tennessee, Jack Daniel's owner Lem Motlow, he was determined to wait Prohibition out (although Motlow faced the added challenge of Tennessee going dry in 1909). Beam turned to farming and quarrying, bided his time, and was vindicated when the 21st Amendment repealed the 18th in 1933.

Another thing Beam had in common with Motlow is both rebuilt the family whiskey business as senior citizens. Beam was aged 70 when he set out to recreate the family yeast strain and to find a shuttered distillery to restore. The location he chose was the defunct Murphy Barber Distillery in Clermont, just 15 miles from Bardstown, and Beam bourbon has been made at Clermont ever since. Beam moved fast and was making bourbon again in 1935.

James B. Beam is sometimes referred to as "The Legend" for what he did. Another title and garland he wears is "The Namesake," because the core family brand was changed from Old Tub to Jim Beam in his honor in 1943. The timing was sound, because although James was still alive, his day was passing. A few years later, his son T. Jeremiah Beam, "Jere," was already the one running things day to day. James B. Beam passed away in 1947.

If his father brought the family legacy through Prohibition, it was Jere Beam who built that business into something like the goliath we know it to be today. One of the first steps he took in that direction was also the most famous: getting Beam bourbon distributed to US military installations around the globe. Whether it was at the PX or in the club, US servicemen of those early Cold War years got to know Jim Beam.

That coup led to growing international sales outside the military, which in turn led to the other part of the Jere Beam legacy: buying and reviving the Churchill Downs Distillery in Boston, Kentucky, in 1954. From the start, it was intended to have even more production capacity than Clermont. Although the Clermont plant is the one most associated with the Jim Beam brand and is the place the tourists on the Kentucky Bourbon Trail visit, it is the Boston plant that has been the principal production facility of the Beam empire, from the time it filled its first barrel.

Jere Beam handed the job of master distiller over to Booker Noe in 1965 and retired from any active role at Jim Beam in 1967. He passed in 1977. I address Booker separately, but in the spirit of describing the Beam dynasty, it's worth noting that Noe worked alongside his cousins Baker and David Beam, with Baker in particular functioning as a lieutenant distiller. Baker's Bourbon is named for him.

Arguably the most interesting thing in the Beam dynasty story is the break in its continuity. Sharp observers who look at the family timeline may notice that Booker Noe retired as master distiller in 1992, but his son Fred Noe did not become master distiller until 2007. That gap was covered by Jerry Dalton, the only master distiller of Jim Beam to come from outside the family. His tenure covered the crucial time of the Small Batch era (although the Jim Beam Small Batch Collection was developed by Booker Noe), when Kentucky bourbon was building a reputation as a premium product, laying the groundwork for the Bourbon Boom of the 2010s.

Beam-Suntory does not call much attention to the Dalton era anymore. He doesn't appear on the website and is scarcely mentioned in any of the current literature, but that shouldn't be read as hiding or denying him. When I asked Beam's representatives about Dalton, they were forthcoming. I think this relatively recent silence is really just a matter of the company preferring their storytelling to focus on the Beam family dynasty. In the name of keeping that story simple, they present it as an unbroken chain of succession. My own opinion is the exception that proves the rule is a fascinating nugget, and Dalton's stint took place at a time in bourbon history too crucial to ever pass over without comment. Dalton retired early to care for his ailing wife and was inducted into the Kentucky Bourbon Hall of Fame in 2023.

His successor brought the title of master distiller back into the family, as Booker's son Fred became the seventh generation of Beam to take over as family distiller in 2007. Although Fred hasn't technically retired yet, his son Freddie (nicknamed "Little Book" by his grandfather) was named master distiller as well in 2022, cementing his status as the eighth-generation family distiller and heir.

Yet even as a family that made a colossal volume of bourbon and built a world-beating brand on it, the Beam dynasty is not limited just to the family business. Their fingerprints can be found all over the Kentucky bourbon industry. Moreover, the Beams are as prevalent in Kentucky bourbon, outside of the Beam company, in modern times as they were historically.

There is a brand owned by Luxco called Minor Case, which refers to Minor Case Beam, a grandson of David Beam (and thus a cousin of James B. Beam). David M. Beam's brother John "Jack" Beam founded the Early Times Distillery, which was later run by his son Edward Beam. Most prominently, a whole wing of the Beam family had their own separate dynasty in operating the Heaven Hill distillery, ending with Craig Beam stepping down as master distiller there in 2015. Today, Stephen and Paul Beam run Limestone Branch, while Craig Beam has returned to the bourbon industry at the new Jackson Purchase Distillery. The irony there is that a branch of the family not actually bearing the name "Beam" has hands on the tiller at the original family business, while their cousins with the name Beam are off doing bourbon elsewhere.

WHISKEY DYNASTIES
NOT NAMED BEAM

Compared to the Beams, most bourbon dynasties, indeed whiskey dynasties in general, are of more recent origins. Take the Russells of Wild Turkey, for example. Jimmy Russell's father was a distillery worker, but never the master distiller. Eddie Russell was the youngest of three sons and was working at Wild Turkey for almost a quarter century before he succeeded his father as master distiller. As is often the case, nobody handed him the top slot. He had to earn it. When he did, a true Wild Turkey-Russell dynasty was formed, and now that dynasty is moving forward: Eddie's son Bruce was made an associate blender in 2022 and collaborated with his father and grandfather on Wild Turkey Generations Bourbon in 2023.

With dynasties so pervasive in Kentucky, one wonders when the next generation of the Samuels clan will start making appearances in Maker's Mark press releases. At Heaven Hill, the Shapiras are now in the third generation of running the family business, even if the Beams no longer make whiskey for them. Whiskey as a family trade is not limited to just Kentucky. In the sister state of Tennessee, Chris Fletcher became master distiller at Jack Daniel's in 2020, following in the footsteps of his grandfather Frank "Frog" Bobo, Lynchburg's fifth master distiller from 1966 to 1988.

One needs to go overseas to find dynasties that approach the seven, presumably eight generations of Beams working in the whiskey trade, but none actually surpass them for longevity. The Grants of Ballindalloch (so named to distinguish them from other Grants in the Scotch whisky trade) have owned and operated Glenfarclas Distillery for six generations. Gordon & MacPhail, the independent bottler of Scotch whisky, was founded in 1895 by the Urquharts and has been a family business ever since. To explore the many Scottish family whisky firms that have lasted for three, four, or five generations could easily make for its own book.

Shinjiro Torii may not have opened the Yamazaki Distillery until 1923, but his first whisky brand was started in 1919 and his liquor company in 1899, so the Toriis and drink go back to the dawn of the 20th century. Nowadays, his grandson Shingo

Torii is a Suntory vice president and the master blender, while his great-grandson Nobuhiro Torii is Suntory's COO.

Ireland has its own current dynasty in the Teelings. John Teeling was an economist, academic, and investment analyst, and despite being a teetotaler, he studied the potential of the Irish whiskey market while working on his doctorate at Harvard in the early 1970s. He took the plunge in 1987, opening Cooley Distillery, then only the third working distillery on the Emerald Isle. In 2007, he revived Kilbeggan, which became only the fourth working distillery in Ireland at the time. In 2012, he sold Cooley and Kilbeggan to Beam Suntory, and by 2015 he had opened another new whiskey-making plant, Great Northern Distillery.

While all this was going on, John Teeling's sons Jack and Stephen had cut their teeth working for him at Cooley, and later ventured out on their own to found the Teeling Whiskey Company in 2012. Initially starting with whiskeys sourced from Cooley (and possibly other distilleries), in 2015 the Teeling brothers won the race to open the first new distillery in Dublin in 125 years.

Just because there is a dynasty doesn't mean nepotism automatically follows. The story of these family trades is one of starting at the bottom and spending one or two decades working up to a senior position or branching off on one's own. The romance of it all is found in the simple truth that maturing whiskey takes years, and in many cases the cask laid down today is intended to become something that your son or even your grandniece might open and work with down the road. As the craft movement has brought many American families back to whiskey making, and whisky distilleries have sprouted up from Sweden to South Africa, I expect to see the concept of whiskey as a family trade take root all around the globe by mid-century.

WHY GEORGE WASHINGTON FIGURES IN SO MANY WHISKEY TALES

If bourbon and rye are quintessentially American spirits, then it only makes sense that George Washington figures into so many whiskey tales. That began in 1753, when Washington was just a 21-year-old militia officer and undertaking his first mission into the wilderness of the Ohio Country, a mission that would lead to Washington ordering the first shots of what became the French and Indian War. That same year, a Mennonite farmer named John Shenk settled near Schaefferstown, Pennsylvania.

Like many enterprising farmers of that era, Shenk became a farmer-distiller. According to folklore, his rye was not only purchased to supply the Revolutionary Army, but General Washington (now very advanced in his military career) himself came to Shenk's farm to do some of the purchasing work. As the tale goes, this whiskey warmed the troops enduring the brutal winter quarters at Valley Forge. What is known for sure is Shenk's distilling business thrived, and he was soon making whiskey for many local farmers who did not own stills of their own. Abe Bomberger bought that distillery in 1861, which ever since has been known as Bomberger's Distillery, and later gave rise to Michter's Whiskey. Michter's, in turn, embraced that Revolutionary folklore as part of its marketing, which continues at the modern, Kentucky-based company. In recent times, Shenk's name is commemorated in a Michter's brand.

But serving as his own commissary agent wasn't Washington's only encounter with whiskey. Washington was also a farmer-distiller, albeit on a much larger scale than Shenk. In addition to his talents as a politician and military man, George Washington was a shrewd businessman as well, always looking to buck the period's trend of indebted farmer-gentlemen in Virginia. At its peak, Washington's distillery was equipped with five stills producing 11,000 gallons of spirit annually. This is at a time when many of Washington's peers in Virginia might make 650 gallons per year. Today, Mount Vernon is engaged in making whiskey, faithfully reproducing Washington's enterprise.

It was proto-industrial distillers like Washington that Alexander Hamilton had in mind, in fact, when he proposed the Whiskey Tax of 1791. Really a tax on distilled spirits production generally, it was nevertheless the first federal tax on a domestic product and was enormously unpopular with the small farmer-distillers of the Western frontier. The frontiersmen's grievances were legitimate, as the law favored the operations of bigger distillers like Washington.

Opposition to the law turned violent in Western Pennsylvania, in what would become known as the Whiskey Rebellion. Washington ordered the raising of a militia army, and at one point led it in person, the first and last time a sitting US president put on the uniform and took personal charge of military forces.

One of those violent incidents was when a German immigrant farmer, Philip Wigle, assaulted a tax collector. After the rebellion ran out of steam and most of the rebels went home, Wigle was one of just two men to find himself arrested, tried, and convicted of treason. He was sentenced to hang, but Washington pardoned both Wigle and his fellow convict. Today, Pittsburgh's Wigle Whiskey commemorates the hard-punching rebel who ran afoul of the first President.

THE BOOKER LEGEND

Whenever I'm talking with a fellow Kentuckian—one who is old enough to remember the days when bourbon was decidedly not cool—about the current boom times, Booker Noe inevitably comes up. These talks dwell on Booker's role in reviving Kentucky bourbon so much that I am usually the one who has to say, "Jimmy Russell was part of that, too, you know."

The fixation on Noe is easily forgiven because it is one so easy to understand. Standing 6'4" tall, Noe was a folksy, gregarious man with a larger than life personality. More than any other person, he invented the modern task of a master distiller as the foremost ambassador of a brand, paving the way for the rockstar status that position often enjoys today. Such a man drops stories in his wake, like leaves whipped away in a stiff breeze, so much so that I could probably add an illustrative Booker Noe story to most of the themes touched on in this book.

For example, elsewhere in the book I delve into natural disasters and major accidents in world whiskey (see page TK). In April 1974, Booker and some of his team were making rounds and tasting samples drawn from different warehouses. When they went inside, it was an overcast day and things were unusually dark out, but they paid no mind. It began raining, but any other sign of what was transpiring was smothered by the industrial distillery noise all around them. They emerged to find that a major tornado had ripped through the property. Almost immediately, they saw a 60-foot-tall barrel escalator knocked over. As they checked the damage, they found five rickhouses had their roofs torn off, and one rickhouse holding over 5,000 barrels was obliterated. In talking about the tornado afterwards, Booker would say that if the twister had turned right instead of left, he and everyone at that sampling meeting would have been under the ruins of something like what remained of the ripped apart Rickhouse J.

Tales of food and Booker abound. Booker was always cooking something for everyone. This ranged from frying a few dozen eggs for breakfast and sharing it out with whoever was there to barbecuing the clutch of fish he caught over the weekend. He smoked his own hams and would often bring them on business trips to Chicago to show restaurateurs how it should be done. Meat from the Noe family smokehouse continues to be a sought-after treat to this day.

But in terms of being a master distiller, his singular contribution is the bourbon that bears him name: Booker's. Developed in 1987 and initially labeled Booker's True Barrel Bourbon, it reflected the barrel selection he favored and was bottled the way he drank it: cask strength, hovering around 125 proof. This whiskey was the last of a string of seminal moves in the 1980s that collectively paved the way for the bourbon industry to climb out of the hole that the 1970s had thrown it into. If Maker's Mark positioned bourbon as a potentially premium product, Elijah Craig opened the door to small batch bourbon with age statements (although some say it was Booker Noe himself who invented the term "small batch"), and Blanton's invented the single barrel, then Booker's gave us cask strength bourbon as we know it today.

Booker's success with his eponymous bourbon led to his development of three other premium bourbons, introduced in 1992: Knob Creek, Basil Hayden, and Baker's, that last one named after his cousin and lieutenant, Baker Beam. The four bourbons were brought together and called the Small Batch Collection. In the mid-1990s, if a bar stocked one, they generally had all four, and it was not uncommon to find them together in a branded bar shelf display case. He retired as master distiller in 1992 but continued to work as a brand ambassador for years after, although I doubt Booker would have called that part work. Noe passed away in 2004.

The only substantial change to Booker's namesake bourbon since has been the decision to denote its individual batches upon release, giving each its own title. These titles are often inspired by stories about Booker Noe or people that he worked with. Among my colleagues, it is sometimes mused that Beam is one day going to run out of ideas for naming Booker's in this way or at least they will start repeating themselves. In the long run, sure they will, but this is Booker Noe we're talking about. It will take them a while to exhaust that particular source of material.

OLD TAYLOR, THE ORIGINAL BOURBON TRAIL DESTINATION

Nowadays, a bourbon distillery that is not open to visitors is an oddity. A few such places are around, but not many, and most of the new distilleries built during the modern Bourbon Boom were designed with tourism in mind. That was not the case when I first began paying attention to the bourbon industry in the late 1980s. In that era, the situation was reversed: only a few Kentucky distilleries were open to visitors, and of those, only Maker's Mark really seemed visitor friendly. Yet the place that first sparked my curiosity about bourbon, Old Taylor, was clearly built from the ground up for visitors. I knew nothing about it, but instantly saw that even a madman wouldn't erect a Victorian castle with the intention of keeping it a secret.

Old Taylor lies alongside Glenn's Creek, and that watercourse seems to wind its way through bourbon's story. Chapter 1 was with Dr. James Crow in the first half of the 19th century. Chapter 2 began when Colonel E. H. Taylor built his showcase for bourbon in 1887.

A descendant of two American presidents, James Madison and Zachary Taylor, Edmund Haynes Taylor Jr. is one of those nondistillers without which it would be impossible to imagine bourbon as it is today. Taylor was initially a banker, but being a banker in the Bluegrass of the 19th century meant one could get quite a lot of exposure to the inner workings of the bourbon business. He was also a skilled politician, and served as the mayor of Frankfort, Kentucky, for 16 years. Bourbon and politics came together in Taylor's single most important contribution. He was a major force in getting the Bottled-in-Bond Act of 1897 passed, a pivotal step in protecting the identity of Kentucky bourbon at a time when you could put vodka flavored with prune juice in a bottle and call it fine old bourbon whiskey.

Old Taylor was his second distillery. Taylor's first was a little place he bought in 1869, on the banks of the Kentucky River outside of Frankfort. He renamed it Old Fire Copper (OFC) but ran into financial difficulties and sold it to a man named George T. Stagg in 1879. Today, that distillery is called Buffalo Trace.

Whereas OFC (and other distilleries in which Taylor owned shares) were existing concerns, Old Taylor was built from the ground up to match Taylor's aristocratic, genteel vision of bourbon's potential image, and to convey that image to consumers and investors. According to the Filson Historical Society, it was "the first distillery in the United States designed and operated as a showplace, combining customer hospitality with the production of spirit." The stillhouse's turreted, castle-like image is more than mere facade. That part of the building is constructed from limestone blocks. The grounds included ornate gardens, and on the banks of Glenn's Creek sat a neoclassical springhouse. All of this was a reasonable carriage ride from Frankfort, a perfect trip for anyone who happened to be in Kentucky's capital.

Old Taylor looked pretty and made whiskey until shuttered by Prohibition. It reopened in the 1930s, but production closed again in 1972. The property was allowed to fall into disrepair, although the rickhouses were used by Jim Beam to store barrels well into the 1980s. That was the state of things when I found the place as a high school student.

With the Bourbon Boom, a story as good as Taylor's and a facility with the potential of Old Taylor were ripe for renewal. Buffalo Trace makes a brand of specialty whiskeys named for Colonel E. H. Taylor, while Old Taylor became Castle & Key in 2014. After extensive renovations, whiskey distilling resumed at the site, and it has once again became an exemplar for Taylor's genteel vision of bourbon. The first in-house Castle & Key bourbon was released in 2022.

GROUND ZERO FOR PAPPY FEVER

When I first put pen to paper and wrote about whiskey, it was possible to stroll into certain liquor stores in Kentucky, put your name on a waiting list, and snag a bottle of Pappy Van Winkle 15 Year Old at regular retail price either that year or the next. Accomplishing that feat today requires calling in some serious favors with someone in the distribution chain or maybe some corruption, as was discovered in Oregon's state liquor control board in early 2023. To buy that bottle on demand in the retail market will, as I write this, set you back about $3,000.

How we got here is a story that has all the twists and turns of being in the bourbon business of the late 20th century. Julian Van Winkle II, son of the very real Pappy Van Winkle, had been making whiskey under contract at the Stitzel-Weller Distillery in Shively, a suburb of Louisville, since the early 1970s. He owned a brand at that point, but not a distillery, and the timing coincided with the whiskey bust of that decade. Whiskey stock sat on ricks for longer due to declining demand, growing ever older. This was true not just with Van Winkle's bourbon, but across the industry.

That was just one of the happy accidents that contributed to the ambrosia-like legend of Pappy Van Winkle. For starters, a combination of production factors (mash, yeast, warehousing, etc.) gave Stitzel-Weller an excellent wheated bourbon, one

that is ever more dearly prized by bourbon collectors. That bourbon aged well during decades-long periods (not all bourbon does). Pappy Van Winkle 20 Year Old was introduced in the early 1990s, around the same time that the Small Batch era came into being, with brands like Knob Creek and Rare Breed.

Once it came into existence, three things cemented Pappy Van Winkle as an excellent bourbon among aficionados: it was extraordinarily good, it had very high age statements attached as a matter of course, and there was never very much of the stuff going around.

But the first plank on that platform of success was based on Stitzel-Weller bourbon, and that distillery closed in 1992. The brand started contract production with Buffalo Trace in 2002, and in between sourced additional stocks of wheated bourbon from Bernheim Distillery. What exactly has been in a bottle of Pappy Van Winkle has changed over time, as the age of the different sources has grown and those sources have been depleted. Buffalo Trace master distiller Harlen Wheatley once told me that some Stitzel-Weller sourced bourbon had been stored away in stainless steel tanks, stopping its aging and freezing it in time. Even so, thirty years on from the closure of Stitzel-Weller, it is a good guess that Van Winkle bourbon is now squarely based on Buffalo Trace's wheated bourbon for all but its oldest expression, the 23 Year Old. That timeline underscores just how irrational the fevered pursuit for Pappy Van Winkle has become.

FOUR GRAND FOR PAPPY IS CHICKEN FEED

While Americans complain bitterly about how the official retail price on a bottle of Pappy Van Winkle 23 Year Old is merely $300, but they are likely to pay north of $4,000 to actually get one, Van Winkle is just a minnow when it comes to expensive and collectable whiskeys. Pappy Van Winkle 23 Year Old doesn't even break into the top ten for most expensive bourbons anymore, let alone most expensive whiskeys in the world. Lately, that latter and most supreme crown is reserved for something Japanese.

As I write this, the most expensive bottle available at retail (I'm deliberately excluding auctions) is Yamazaki 55 Year Old, which at the time of writing commanded a retail average of $884,281. For the last several years, the top 10 list for the world's most expensive whiskies has been dominated either by some seriously old Japanese single malts or releases from The Macallan's ultra-aged Lalique series. There was a reason that when burglars knocked over Maison du Whisky in Paris, they went straight for the Japanese bottles.

The Japanese whisky industry had tried repeatedly to succeed in international markets since the Second World War, but it really achieved this only after *Whisky Bible* author Jim Murray declared The Yamazaki Single Malt Sherry Cask 2013 as the best whisky in the world in his 2014 edition. That move garnered international headlines, pulling major attention from the drinking public at large onto Japanese whisky. But the larger truth is that Japanese whisky as a category had been quietly building acclaim among experts in the years prior. Nonetheless, having a Japanese malt declared best in the world by the drink's top review tome started a fever with aficionados and collectors, which became a boomerang for the industry. On the one hand, Japanese whisky finally had its long sought-after international acclaim. Yet that came at a cost, namely that Japanese whisky as a whole was at risk of being drunk dry.

For a decade now, drinkers in the US have been fretting over a "bourbon shortage," but this has never truly materialized. Shortages are about not being able to get things at all or seeing prices for the commodity at large skyrocket to compensate for the aforementioned scarcity, not having to make mildly inconvenient choices. Excepting whiskeys made at Buffalo Trace and the brief rye whiskey supply crunch of 2011 and 2012, "shortage" has never accurately described the general availability of American whiskey.

To see what a real shortage is, look at Japan, which badly depleted its stocks of aged whiskies in the drive to achieve that international renown. Between 2015 and 2020, Nikka was forced to discontinue twenty expressions with age statements. Suntory took a different approach: in 2015, they raised prices on their whiskies by 20 to 25 percent across the board, and those whiskies have continued to see regular, sharp price increases since.

So, the inflated prices commanded by whiskies from Japan are not confined just to expressions that are slightly older than

I am. Ten years ago, I could get the good, but solidly entry-level Yamazaki 12 Year Old single malt for about $85; today, I would expect to pay at least $150. On Nikka's end of thing, Yoichi 10 Year Old single malt was only reintroduced in April 2023, but at a staggering $175 a bottle. Japanese whisky is only now showing the barest, most initial signs of catching up with demand, and that after a decade of being caught in a supply crunch.

STEALING WHISKEY

Back in 2009, I read a celebrated book called *The Billionaire's Vinegar*, about a scam involving a bottle of wine supposedly owned by Thomas Jefferson. Rare booze, it seems, attracts crime in the way that anything valuable and portable will. Whiskey is no exception, and old, rare, in demand whiskeys from around the world continue to remain scarce and command inflated prices. As a consequence, those bottles (and sometimes whole casks) lie at the center of many heists, corrupt machinations, and scams.

As I write this, the most recent and highest profile example saw top managers at the Oregon Liquor and Cannabis Control Commission (OLCC) under investigation for using their power to divert bottles of Pappy Van Winkle and other rare whiskeys away from the general public, so they could buy them at regular retail prices. This and other allegations of irregularities led to the 2023 resignation of the OLCC director, Steve Marks, and at least one other top official. But whiskey crime is hardly a new phenomenon.

The Chicago Outfit Hijacks Bourbon: If one is delving into the subject of whiskey theft, it's really only appropriate to begin with the Mafia. In December 1957, a truck bound from Louisville to Chicago was carrying 875 cases of whiskey when it was hijacked. Almost half of those cases were later found in Chicago's Café Continental, owned by connected guys Gerald Covelli and David Falzone. Most of the remaining cases were tied to other mob-run establishments, and the hijack was worth about half a million dollars in today's money (similar to the destroyed value when a Jack Daniel's truck overturned on the interstate in Tennessee in 2021).

Covelli and Falzone were connected to several murders and disappearances; the hostess of the Continental was Covelli's girlfriend, and later became his wife after the murder of her husband. They were brought to trial for the whiskey hijacking in 1959, which resulted in a hung jury voting 11 to 1. The holdout, Robert Saporito, later confessed to being paid by his brother, an ex-Chicago police officer, to vote not guilty. Covelli later pled guilty to a charge of jury tampering in the case.

The Great Paris Whisky Robbery: The most lucrative whisky crime I'm aware of is 2017's robbery of La Maison du Whisky in Paris. The French adore whisky, and La Maison du Whisky has the reputation of being one of the best whisky stores in the world. In this well-planned heist, the thieves made off with 69 bottles of what is now the rarest class of whisky in the world: very old Japanese whisky. Their haul was worth over $800,000.

Pappygate: Most infamous among bourbon enthusiasts is the legendary Pappygate, because it was easily the most reported upon whiskey crime of the early 21st century. In 2013, routine inventory checks at Buffalo Trace uncovered that they were missing over 200 bottles of Pappy Van Winkle, a stainless steel storage barrel of Eagle Rare 17 Year Old, and other items. Further investigation led to Buffalo Trace employee Gilbert "Toby" Curtsinger, who turned out to be leading a ring of ten others, many of whom were employed at other distilleries. The ring was centered on a softball team. They had also stolen bourbon from Wild Turkey and were engaged in dealing illegal steroids. Curtsinger's crew flipped on him, so he was the only one who went to prison over Pappygate, and he served only one month of his sentence after being granted shock probation. So, the most infamous story of whiskey crime in modern American history ended with the barest of whimpers.

The Sad Tale of the Old Farm Pure Rye Thief: When former model Pat Hill set out to turn an old mansion into the Pittsburgh area South Broadway Manor Bed and Breakfast, she found over one hundred bottles of Old Farm Pure Rye Whiskey hidden under a flight of stairs. This whiskey was made in 1912, believed to be part of a collection that belonged to Henry Frick (owner of Old Overholt and partner of Andrew Mellon, later secretary of the Treasury) and famed industrialist Andrew Carnegie. Imagine Hill's horror when she later discovered 52 of the bottles had been emptied. She pointed the finger at John Saunders, her caretaker. The 62-year-old's DNA was all over the bottles, and since he was being accused of stealing and drinking $102,400 worth of pre-Prohibition rye, he was arrested in 2013. The case never went anywhere, though, as Saunders passed away the next year.

WHISKEY THIEVES

The whiskey thief I address here is cut from a different cloth. Or better to say, cut from a different sheet of copper.

Copper is very much part of the romance of whiskey making, such is the beauty of the thing. For even the smallest craft distiller, the hybrid pot-column still is routinely the centerpiece of their establishment, and anyone operating stainless steel equipment is usually embarrassed by the comparison.

A handful of enthusiasts might have a little of that romance in their home, what with stove-top scale alembic stills being a (dangerous, potentially explosive) thing. More often than not, those of us whiskey lovers who want a little of that copper to decorate the home pick up a different tool of the trade, the whiskey thief.

This is the standard tool of the industry for extracting samples out of the bunghole of a cask. The thief is a tube coming to a conical nub at one end, and with holes on both ends. The tube is inserted into the cask, the back hole is capped with the thumb, and suction traps the liquid inside. Once removed from the barrel, whiskey can be poured into beakers or glasses simply by uncapping the thumb from the back hole. Most companies engaged in building stills also make whiskey thieves. Vendome in Louisville, America's premier still fabricator, will sell you a fine copper whiskey thief for $390.

If whiskey has been aging for decades, extracting a sample may not be as easy as popping the bung and inserting the thief. The real thieves are the angels, and a barrel might not have much left in it after they've been by to claim their share, year upon year. When there are only a few gallons left, you may need to pick the barrel up onto one barrel rim and roll it around to extract a good sample. That isn't easy, as I can attest to from hands-on experience. Empty, a bourbon barrel weighs about 125 pounds.

If the whiskey thief is the trade tool for extracting liquid from barrels, distillery workers had their own unofficial tools for thieving a little whiskey off the job for their own consumption. In America, this was often as simple as a rubber hose, but in Scotland and Ireland they used a simplified whiskey thief called a dipping dog. This was a copper tube, small enough to keep in the pocket or wear around the neck on a chain.

Whiskey thieves don't need to be made of copper. I have seen some made of glass, and food grade plastic or stainless steel would do the job just as well. But as I wrote when I started, copper is very much part of the romance of whiskey making, stainless steel is plain, and only kinksters find anything romantic about plastic.

BLANTON'S: BOURBON COMES OUT OF THE GATE

Once an accessible premium expression, Blanton's Bourbon has become another rarely seen, frustratingly hard-to-get expression from Buffalo Trace Distillery. The brand even became the centerpiece of a 2023 investigation into what was suspected to be illegal re-importation scheme: one of America's best-known dealers in collectable whiskeys, Justins' House of Bourbon, was discovered with a substantial inventory of Blanton's that found its way back to a DC warehouse after being exported to the European market. The company was later cleared of all wrongdoing except for poor recordkeeping.

In one sense, that scarcity is just another part of the story of how the fever for products even marginally related to Pappy Van Winkle has consumed Buffalo Trace Distillery and whatever it makes. But that scarcity is also the culmination of how Blanton's, some four decades after its introduction, succeeded wildly beyond the ambitions of its creator.

Rewind to 1984, when the Kentucky bourbon industry was in the doldrums following the Great Whiskey Bust of the 1970s. This was a time when many in the business were looking for ways to revive bourbon. Maker's Mark made its major international marketing push, Heaven Hill would introduce Elijah Craig 12 Year Old, and both these bourbons would be labeled as part of the "small batch" category several years later.

Elmer T. Lee, the master distiller at what was then called the George T. Stagg Distillery, brought two threads together in his answer to bourbon's problem. First, he looked at the success the Scotch whisky industry was having in marketing single malt whiskies as a premium product. Lee also recalled how his mentor, Albert Blanton, would entertain his guests (business or otherwise) with so-called "honey barrels" drawn from the center floors of Warehouse H. That warehouse differs from the masonry rickhouses at Buffalo Trace in that it is clad in metal sheeting, less well-insulated, and therefore more susceptible to changes in weather.

Lee pinned his idea on the word "single," choosing to bottle his new brand from individual barrels instead of batches drawn from dozens or hundreds of barrels. This new concept was the single barrel bourbon. He drew from Blanton's stock of honey barrels, named the brand after his mentor, and then went looking for packaging that expressed the bourbon's prestige.

That final point came in the form of Blanton's eye-catching globe bottle, wax seal, and horse-and-jockey stopper. The last feature is a nod to that other signature Bluegrass industry, horse breeding and racing. Starting in 1999, they began using eight different figures atop their bottles, each of the eight presenting a different stride. Collecting all eight presents a horse running a race, from standing start to crossing the finish line.

If the ghost stories surrounding Buffalo Trace are true, then Blanton watched over his namesake bourbon closely. He passed away in the Stony Point mansion on the property, a building that now serves as offices. Apparitions of Blanton have been seen around the distillery and—and in particular, the mansion—ever since.

EVAN WILLIAMS, TRUE PIONEER

On the Evan Williams website, there is a page devoted to the current distillers behind the brand (and much else from Heaven Hill). This list is headed by a not-so-current figure, the brand namesake, and his entry reads:

"Evan Williams was a natural-born leader, innovator, and entrepreneur. He worked in numerous trades as a businessman, politician, and—most notably—whiskey distiller. In 1783, he founded Kentucky's first commercial distillery on the banks of the Ohio River. Many years and barrels later, our master distillers are still producing Bourbon the right way, using the same time-honored methods."

That is a more careful summation of the Evan Williams story, because I recall a time when the story in circulation named Williams as Kentucky's first *bourbon* distiller. That claim was repeated by a teacher I had in high school, no less. A few years later, when I had learned a little more about the bourbon business, the thing that made me smirk about the tale was that Heaven Hill also made Elijah Craig, another man regarded as the originator of bourbon.

The modern and official version sticks to the facts. Williams was a Welsh immigrant, who arrived in Louisville in 1780. At that time Williams was 25 and Louisville itself (named for King Louis XVI, because the Revolutionary War was going on at the time) had been around for just two years. The distillery he established in 1783 was different from others in what was then the westernmost county of Virginia in that it was wholly commercial in nature.

Most distillers in this era, before there was a United States (or even a Kentucky, for that matter), were farmer-distillers. They grew their grain crops, kept what they needed for seed, animal feed, and food for the family, and turned the rest into whiskey. Compared to grain or flour, whiskey is both more portable and has a longer shelf life. Often these farmer-distillers would use their equipment to make whiskey for other farmers, as well (Jacob Beam is an example), but the cornerstone of the operation was making a product out of their own agricultural produce.

Williams did not have a farm, and instead bought corn from local farmers. Although his operation was small compared to the rum distillers of Boston or that of George Washington, his 1801 federal license indicated he had three stills, each of which would have been the same size as the one still most farmer-distillers owned around the region. He bought grain, made whiskey, put it in barrels, and shipped it down the Ohio River.

The Williams story is often told to play up his role as a civic leader in Louisville. As a stone mason and builder, he erected the first jail and courthouse in Jefferson County. Williams also served on the town's board (its de facto city council) for a time, and was made its first wharfmaster in 1797. But he was also indicted for selling whiskey without a license in 1788. At least as embarrassing is that while Williams was serving as wharfmaster, he was condemned by other city officials for the way he was disposing of his stillage and wastewater into the river.

So yes, Williams was absolutely the first distiller to operate a whiskey-making business in Kentucky that wasn't an adjunct to being a farmer. But as for the older stories about Williams inventing bourbon, accounts I heard forty years ago, there is no proof anyone was even using the term bourbon at the time of his death in 1810.

ELIJAH CRAIG: WHEN THE REAL STORY IS BETTER THAN THE LEGEND

Elijah Craig is a classic example in American whiskey making of a brand named after a real person, but most of the stories told about that real person are fable, not fact. The real Elijah Craig was born in the Virginia Colony, but when exactly is an open question; sources say 1738, 1745, and 1748, a spread of uncertainty that puts the dispute over when Jack Daniel was born in the shade. That blurriness regarding the events of Elijah Craig's life is, in fact, the central characteristic of his story. He was known to have become a Baptist in the 1760s and ordained as a minister in either 1770 or 1771.

What isn't blurry is that being an active Baptist, never mind a preacher, in colonial Virginia was a ticket to trouble. It is often forgotten that one of the reasons freedom of religion is enshrined in the Bill of Rights is that some of the colonies had their own government-sanctioned brand of Protestantism. Virginia was one of these; the official church was Anglicanism, and nonconforming evangelicals were basically regarded as miscreant criminals. Craig was arrested and jailed twice, in Orange and Culpeper counties.

This religious persecution is what led the Reverend Craig to settle in the Bluegrass, although the circumstances are, again, hazy. Accounts differ on whether he led the "Traveling Church," a group of several hundred Baptists migrating from Virginia across the Cumberland Gap to the Kentucky frontier, or merely accompanied his brothers on the journey. What is known is that he came to own 1,000 acres in what would become Scott County, Kentucky, by the late 1780s and got down to work. He laid out the town of Lebanon, which became Georgetown in 1790 (renamed to honor George Washington), and that town eventually became the county seat. He is credited with many business ventures, such as Kentucky's first paper mill, a sawmill, a gristmill, and a ferry across the Kentucky River, among others. Craig was also a prominent educator, opening a school that would become Rittenhouse Academy, which in turn was the forerunner of the modern Georgetown College.

Like many farmers of the era, Craig also got into the business of turning his surplus corn into whiskey. Where legend enters the story is the claim that Elijah Craig is the "father of Kentucky bourbon." I've heard three versions of how Craig came to invent the key practice of aging bourbon in charred oak barrels over the years. The first was that as a Baptist and a businessman, Craig was a notorious cheapskate, and he charred the insides of the barrels to recycle them from other purposes into bourbon containers. Another version is the barrels were charred in a barn fire, and the last version is that he was somehow armed with knowledge of how the French were aging cognac.

Yet none of these stories has any supporting evidence, and the very claim that Craig invented bourbon has been traced back to an unsourced assertion in Richard Collins' 1874 *History of Kentucky*. Craig certainly made whiskey, as court records show he owed back taxes under the same federal excise act that sparked the Whiskey Rebellion. But not only is there no proof that Craig invented bourbon, it is highly likely the whiskey he made wasn't even recognizable as bourbon. The first written reference to bourbon whiskey wasn't printed until 13 years after Craig's death.

Nonetheless, the story from the late 19th century stuck, and when Heaven Hill was looking for a way out of the slump that followed the Great Whiskey Bust of the 1970s, they settled on creating a 12 year old bourbon made in small batches and naming it after Elijah Craig. Introduced in 1984, it was one of those seminal expressions, a peer of Blanton's and Booker's, that helped pick the Kentucky bourbon industry up off the floor and open the way to the modern bourbon boom.

The story of a Baptist preacher inventing bourbon—considering the Baptists would later become so closely associated with the temperance movement—is only the beginning of the irony

ELIJAH CRAIG

KENTUCKY STRAIGHT
BOURBON WHISKEY

47% vol.   70 cl.

Years **12**

PRODUCT OF U.S.A.

240-3425

in the Craig story. Scott County, where he built his distillery, was dry until 2012. So, you couldn't buy bourbon in its legendary birthplace, but there was a liquor store sitting right across the Scott-Fayette county line. As a teenager, I briefly attended Georgetown College, and a campus legend spoke of how some barrels of Craig's original whiskey were tucked away inside the columns of Giddings Hall. That is probably just another bit of Craig folklore, since Giddings Hall was built in 1838, long after the Reverend's passing.

BOARDWALK EMPIRE, THE SECRETARY, AND PENNSYLVANIA RYE

When James Cromwell appeared in the HBO series *Boardwalk Empire*, he took a relatively small part and captured so much attention that I spent the weeks following the premiere fielding a steady trickle of questions about the real story behind Andrew Mellon and his ties to whiskey and 1920s bootlegging. That is a testament not only to Cromwell's talent as an actor, but also to how obscure of a brand Old Overholt had become. After all, the glowering face of Abraham Overholt still adorns every label, staring at you from store and bar shelves. In those dozen or so inquiries, nobody ever thought to ask about him. It's a dismaying truth when one realizes Old Overholt is the oldest continuously maintained whiskey brand in America, dating back to 1810.

The 18th and 19th century story of the Overholts mirrors that of the Beam family in most respects. They were also German immigrants who Anglicized their name and transitioned from being farmer-distillers to commercial distillers. The main distinction was the Overholts made rye in Pennsylvania, not bourbon in Kentucky. Abraham Overholt died in 1870, and the company passed to his grandson Henry Clay Frick. It was Frick who brought Andrew Mellon in as a partner. Frick died in 1919, the year the 18th Amendment passed, and left his share of Overholt Rye to Mellon. So, Mellon came into a majority ownership of Old Overholt just in time to see the distillery shuttered for Prohibition.

The Mellons were a wealthy and influential Pittsburgh family, and Andrew Mellon entered the family banking business in the 1870s. Buying into Old Overholt was just one of numerous interests he held, either privately or through the bank. In 1921, he was appointed Treasury Secretary, and thus headed the agency that decided which six distilleries would be issued licenses to continue the sale of "medicinal whiskey" under Prohibition. In an example of the kind of flagrant conflict of interest that was typical of Mellon's era, his own Old Overholt got one of those licenses. It was because Overholt was so licensed that Mellon was then able to get a good price on its later sale in 1925. About midway through Prohibition, Mellon divested himself of the whiskey business.

Mellon's self-serving abuse of his authority preserved Old Overholt to a limited extent, but the Pennsylvania whiskey industry as a whole never truly recovered from the battering of Prohibition, the Great Depression, and World War II restrictions.

When the Great Whiskey Bust came in the 1970s, it was the final blow that cemented the slow demise of both the industry and its associated style of making a spicy whiskey with a very high rye content. Old Overholt was acquired by Jim Beam in 1987, and from that point has been made as a sweeter Kentucky style rye. Bomberger's Distillery, the last one operating in Pennsylvania at that time, ceased production just two years later, and Pennsylvania ryes like the original Old Overholt would not rebound until craft distillers started making them again.

THE KING IS DEAD, LONG LIVE THE KING

No other Prohibition era bootlegger better illustrates how intertwined the era's criminal enterprises were with the legitimate booze business than George Remus, the so-called "King of the Bootleggers." This is because while bathtub gin and moonshine were flourishing industries in the 1920s, those production methods left a great deal to be desired. A problem similar to that confronted by the nascent craft whiskey sector today also hampered the Prohibition era's illicit distillers: making whiskey taste the way people want it to demands years of maturation. For the start-up craft distiller, that is a matter of waiting, and the axiom that time is money weighs heavily on them; for the illicit distiller, there was the even heavier issue that law enforcement could show up at any moment and destroy all those expensively aged spirits.

So, some bootleggers were engaged in smuggling whiskies from abroad, mostly from Scotland and Ireland. Others feasted on the piled-high remains of the now shuttered American whiskey industry. Like a fat tick, Remus sucked warehouses of bourbon dry and grew wealthy on the proceeds.

A German immigrant, Remus began his professional life as a pharmacist, but switched to law in his middle twenties and was admitted to the Illinois Bar in 1904. He became a phenomenally successful criminal defense attorney in Chicago, renowned for his courtroom theatrics. Adjusted for inflation, Remus was earning between $6 and $7 million per year around the time Prohibition was enacted. It was through his law practice that Remus saw how much money could be made in bootlegging, because some new clients came from that new and growing criminal business. Studying the Volstead Act, Remus realized he could legally buy and trade in stockpiles of whiskey with the intent to sell to licensed pharmacists, and that four-fifths of the nation's whiskey was warehoused within 300 miles of the city of Cincinnati.

Remus left the law behind (literally and figuratively), moved to Cincinnati, and set up his "Circle" or plan. He bought shuttered distilleries and their inventories; bought wholesale pharmaceutical companies, to have control over dispensing the licenses for medicinal whiskey; and procured the federal withdrawal permits (often through bribery), so he could legally remove whiskey. Up to this point, the Circle led to a mostly legal circumvention of Prohibition, but selling medicinal whiskey was small potatoes. The last step was to use his own trucking companies to haul the whiskey around, and then arrange phony heists where his own men hijacked the trucks. Thus he "stole" the whiskey from himself, it disappeared from his public books, and he then illicitly sold it on as bootleg whiskey. Within a year of starting operations, Remus controlled a third of all whiskey stocks in America.

Abbott Kahler, who wrote *Eden Park* under her pen name Karen Abbott, said of Remus, "George Remus was many things: a poor immigrant, a striver, a brawler, a baller, a brilliant entrepreneur, a fantastic liar, a gentleman, a thief, a murderer, an eccentric madman, a mass of contradictions, a teetotaler, arguably the most successful bootlegger in American history, an inspiration for Jay Gatsby, and the absolute embodiment of Jazz Age culture." He referred to himself in the third person, and never lost his habit of courtroom histrionics. Like Jay Gatsby, Remus scandalously flaunted his wealth, valued at almost $1 billion in today's money. At the end of a 1921 party, he gave each male guest a diamond stickpin or watch, and each lady a new car.

Probably the most ordinary and tawdry part of the Remus story is that he ran off with his much younger legal secretary, Imogene Brown, and eventually divorced his first wife, who levelled charges of abuse against him. Running off with his secretary was where things went wrong for Remus. In 1923, he became a partner in a scheme to loot the inventory of Jack Daniel's in St. Louis, Missouri (where the brand eventually landed after being driven first from Tennessee and then Alabama by state-level Prohibitions). His partners disregarded Remus's advice on how to make off with the whiskey without drawing attention, resulting in Remus and a couple dozen co-conspirators landing in prison in 1925. While Remus was in prison, a Prohibition agent named Franklin Dodge, who had previously been spying on Remus from inside prison, resigned from the bureau and started an affair with Imogene Brown.

Dodge and Brown began liquidating Remus's property empire and hiding the proceeds. They also started a plot to have Remus deported, and when that failed another alleged plot to have him murdered. Imogene filed for divorce and Remus, incandescent, countersued.

Out of prison, Remus sought out Imogene on her way to the courthouse, who fled. A car chase ensued, which ended with Remus pursuing his estranged wife through Eden Park. That was where he shot her in the belly, by the Spring House Gazebo and in front of several witnesses. She died, and Remus turned himself into the police.

In his peculiar manner, Remus declared "Remus will defend himself!" Calling on his past profession, he slandered Brown and Dodge in court as conspirators out to destroy him, while defending himself as suffering from "transitory maniacal insanity." It is often wrongly reported that this was the first use of the temporary insanity plea in an American courtroom, but it was not: Edwin M. Stanton, who would later serve as US Secretary of War during the Civil War, got Congressman Dan Sickles off for murdering his philandering wife by arguing temporary insanity in 1859. Nonetheless, Remus was acquitted, and the acquittal was upheld on appeal. He moved to Covington, Kentucky, across the river from the seat of his lost empire. He died there in 1952, very much out of the limelight.

The legend of George Remus was revived in the hit HBO series *Boardwalk Empire*, which is what inspired Kahler to write her book about him. Following up on that renewed notoriety, MGP keeps the Remus name alive today with a bourbon brand, complete with Art Deco styled bottles.

MAKER'S MARK

Along the Kentucky Bourbon Trail, a traveler will find most of the sites are surprisingly modern. I say surprisingly, because one inevitably ties the making of whiskey to romantic illusions of handicraft carried out by a family's umpteenth generation in the trade, working in facilities that more resemble a barn than a factory. Only sometimes does reality meet that expectation.

Most Kentucky distilleries are industrial facilities. Some, like Angel's Envy and New Riff, are artful fusions of metal and glass, designed with the visitors who flock to them clearly in mind. Others are purely functional, so much so that Wild Turkey is the only example of such a pragmatic place that is open to the general public. A few are still factories, but are decidedly not modern, and so little changed that their industrial-era, yesteryear look endows them with a certain charm. Four Roses and Buffalo Trace are among those that fall into that category.

Only a very few combine the well-aged setting with the intent of being not just a place to make whiskey, but to serve as a showcase for it. And only one of these existed when I was first taking an interest in Kentucky's bourbon heritage. That was Maker's Mark. Until the late 1990s, this was the only place I could take a nonbourbon fan to see how bourbon was made and expect them to enjoy the experience, and there weren't that many bourbon fans around in those days. Everything about Maker's Mark is meant to catch the eye and hold it. For most, that begins and ends at the bottle, but the distillery at Star Hill Farm in Loretto, Kentucky, comes to claim and keep that attention for anyone who visits.

Maker's Mark began as what today might be called an early retirement start-up. Current Maker's Mark CEO Rob Samuels describes it starting out as a "hobby distillery." Bill Samuels Sr., a scion of one of Kentucky's bourbon dynasties, sold the family's T. W. Samuels Distillery in the early 1950s and set out to create a more elevated, approachable bourbon. While Bill

Sr. focused on the production side of things, his wife, Margie, developed the brand identity. Inspired by a visit to Williamsburg, Virginia, the tranquil, anti-industrial atmosphere of Maker's Mark is very much her conception, and bringing people to out-of-the-way Loretto to see the distillery was a major facet of her marketing plan in the 1950s and 1960s.

Whether Maker's Mark is the prettiest distillery in Kentucky depends on the observer, but for my part the answer has shifted around over the last three decades. Lately, I think Maker's has reclaimed that garland, and Margie's vision remains unmarred.

One key choice to maintain that vision was how to govern the swelling count of visitors coming to Star Hill Farm every year. Even as late as the middle 2000s, I was able to take folks who came home to Kentucky with me straight down the access road along Whiskey Creek, park in a gravel lot next to the stillhouse, and join the next tour on the schedule. It was certainly a scenic route, but if that road had to absorb the modern tourist traffic, it would have throttled the distillery's bucolic charm. So, Maker's Mark built the current access road, the first entirely new road constructed in Marion County in 35 years, swinging wide and around the distillery grounds. "It was crucial to the development of the distillery," says Rob Samuels. Nowadays, the old creek-side road is home to shady and secluded cut limestone benches and a mushroom farm.

On the production side of things, Maker's Mark is routinely described as being purposefully inefficient. That hobby distillery nature of things continues on an industrial scale as Maker's Mark has expanded and is even embedded in that expansion.

Rather than simply build successively larger plants (a choice made by almost all of their peers), they've *duplicated* their still apparatus twice now, first in 2005 and again in 2015, with a third duplication/expansion currently slated for construction in the site of that old parking lot. Maker's is not the only distillery to expand by copying their existing setup repeatedly. Bardstown Bourbon Company followed a similar approach. The difference is that while they are very practiced at replicating their production process and hardware now, I doubt very much that Bill Samuels Sr. had any of that in mind when he got started in 1958. Bardstown Bourbon Company had their expansion scheme built into the very plans for their building.

To those who have known the Maker's Mark property since before the Bourbon Boom, the vast scope of the expansion is obvious. Yet many of the hobby distillery features still remain. The hand-dipped wax seals are the most obvious, having been turned into a tourist experience in their own right: visitors can dip their own bottles to take home. Less showy is that they still print their own labels onsite, using the original press made in 1935.

If that plan of action for meeting demand isn't unique to Maker's Mark, other facets of how they make bourbon are. For one thing, they only make one mash bill, and thus one kind of whiskey: wheated bourbon. It is unusual for a big American whiskey distiller to make just the one product nowadays, with even Jack Daniel's diversifying with the introduction of their own rye whiskeys starting in 2012. Buffalo Trace gets showered in glory for making the wheated bourbon that goes into Pappy Van Winkle, but they make three different kinds of bourbon for their many, many brands. Yet Maker's Mark has built their entire identity around wheated bourbon, and their idea of growth is to make more of it, not to make something else as well. That is commitment to a singular craft, and these days their peers in doing just the one thing are the single malt distilleries, some found in America, but mostly in Scotland.

Another unique facet of Maker's Mark is their cellar-aged bourbon. In 2015, dynamite was used to blast a cave out of a limestone hillside adjacent to the distillery, and that cave remains the only purpose-built, underground whiskey aging warehouse in the bourbon industry. The cellar was an outgrowth of another first, Maker's 46, the original bourbon made with a stint of secondary maturation using French oak staves inserted directly into the barrel. In developing Maker's 46, it was discovered that the stave finish worked best over a nine-week period in a cold environment. Initially, Maker's 46 and then also Maker's Mark Private Select were made only during the winter months, constricting output. Building the cellar produced a stable, cool environment for making these stave-insert whiskeys year-round.

MARGIE'S RED WAX SEAL

Folks working at Maker's Mark like to speak of the four "Ws" that go into making a bottle of their bourbon. Three of the four—water, wheat, and wood—were in Bill Samuels' wheelhouse. Only one W is tied to Margie Samuels' contribution in building the brand's identity, wax. But it's that red wax seal, dripping down the neck of the bottle, that is perhaps the single most recognizable part of what Maker's Mark does. One of the maxims about Maker's Mark is that Margie's work is the reason people buy their first bottle, while Bill's work is why they buy their second.

As Rob Samuels tells it, Margie regarded conventional advertising as "rude" (one can only imagine what she would have thought of the series *Mad Men*, given her opinion of their work), so she pinned a lot of her marketing on the look of the bottle. She was a design enthusiast with a knack for collecting, and the inspiration for the wax is said to have come from old cognac bottles. The squared look of the bottle was also inspired by those antique cognac bottles. She applied her chemistry degree and experimented with creating her own process for a wax seal by evicting Bill Jr.'s high school yearbook photo lab from the basement and commandeering the family deep fryer as a vat.

After perfecting the wax and the hand-dipping, Margie and Bill Sr. clashed about actually using it in production. Bill thought it was too complicated and costly for what was essentially a gimmick. The wax dip wasn't actually a practical seal and was effectively decorative. Margie settled the argument by reminding him which one of them graduated first in their respective high school classes. Given his doubts, I can only guess what Bill Sr. would think if he knew that today some 60 workers are employed in hand-dipping Maker's Mark bottles in Margie's red wax.

The fryer Margie used to perfect the red wax is on display at the Samuels House, an early nineteenth-century Georgian brick home located in the hamlet of Samuels, outside of Bardstown, which is available as a charming, if pricey, vacation rental for folks exploring the Kentucky Bourbon Trail. The one on display at the distillery is a replica, so the original is a special treat reserved just for guests of the Samuels family.

SWEAT, BARRELS, AND BOURBON

Three of the aforementioned Ws of Maker's Mark are part of their production process, but their wood has a feature that is unique among the big Kentucky distillers. All the bourbon companies use 53-gallon new oak barrels that have been charred on the inside, but what makes the process at the Star Hill Farm distillery special is that they rotate the barrels.

Depending on the distillery, maturation in charred new oak barrels accounts for between 60 and 90 percent of the end flavor of bourbon, as well as contributing all of the color. At the other Kentucky Majors, a newly filled barrel is lodged in its spot in the rickhouse, and there it stays until it is selected for dumping. How a barrel will mature in a given part of the rickhouse is long understood from experience, and most products are made using recipe-like guides, with X number of barrels drawn from this rickhouse bottom floor, Y from the center-left of that rickhouse top floor, and Z from the right corner of that rickhouse middle floor.

Outlier barrels, the redheaded cuckoos of maturation, are a problem of the process, though. These aren't necessarily bad barrels, just not what was expected. Outliers are usually blended into consistency by drawing anywhere from a few hundred to several hundred barrels. Volume drowns out the odd ducks.

As Rob Samuels often puts it, Bill and Margie started a hobby distillery, and conceived their sense of scale accordingly. Instead of using batches measured in hundreds of thousands of gallons to fashion consistency, Bill Sr. instead wanted all barrels to be consistent. His method for achieving that was also long understood in the 1950s, but rarely used then or since: barrel rotation.

At Maker's, a barrel will spend at least its first three years lodged in the upper floors of the rickhouse. When the tasters decide a barrel has spent enough time cooking in the summer heat, a barrel is then moved to the cooler, lower floors, slowing the maturation. Moving the barrels around in this way exercises a greater control over the outcome in each one. That was how Bill Sr. achieved consistency in his bourbon, and it allowed him to make batches using much smaller barrel dumps, usually around just a dozen barrels. Although Maker's Mark doesn't officially label themselves as such, many experts have called them the original small batch bourbon.

It's easy to imagine this process requiring just the rickhouse workers plus a few extra hands drafted from elsewhere in the company during the 1950s and 1960s, but the commitment to retaining this practice in modern times is staggering. Nowadays, Maker's Mark moves 90,000 barrels per year. For comparison, the single largest rickhouse in Kentucky is owned by Jim Beam and holds 59,000 barrels. Each barrel weighs hundreds of pounds, and their estimate for the sweat involved in annual rotation is 10,800 hours of labor. A team of five experienced hands working full-time would need more than two months to accomplish this. Like so much else at Maker's Mark, sticking with the handicraft ways laid out by Bill Sr. and Margie doesn't come cheap.

HOW MAKER'S MARK DID
WHAT SCOTLAND WOULDN'T

Maker's 46 is part of a worthy story beyond being Maker's first major brand extension in over 50 years or the creation of Kentucky bourbon's only aging cellar. It also underscores some of the cultural differences between bourbon and Scotch whisky, both in their respective industries and among drinkers. Maker's 46 wasn't the first expression based around inserting French oak staves into the barrel; before that was a Scotch whisky called The Spice Tree, which met a fate that would have been impossible in America.

The Spice Tree was a creation of Compass Box, a negociant company founded in 2000 by an American named John Glaser. As a negociant, Compass Box buys whiskies from distilleries around Scotland and creates its own brands using the accumulated stocks. The Spice Tree was created in 2005 by drawing on an idea borrowed from the wine industry, with at least part of the whisky in the blend receiving a period of secondary maturation after heavily toasted new French oak staves were inserted into the existing barrels.

It all went wrong when it ran afoul of the Scotch Whisky Association (SWA). Like the Kentucky Distillers Association (KDA), the SWA is a trade organization, not an arm of either the Scottish or British governments. But unlike its American counterpart, the body exercises considerable regulatory function. In the case of The Spice Tree, in 2006 the SWA decided that because stave inserts had never been used in whisky making before, anything made with this process wasn't really Scotch whisky. The SWA told Compass Box to stop under threat of legal action. Unable to wage an expensive battle in the courts with the SWA, Compass Box found a different means of making The Spice Tree and abandoned their stave inserts.

By contrast, when Maker's Mark used the same process to create Maker's 46 in 2010, nobody opposed it. The KDA leaves it up to federal authorities as to what is or is not bourbon whiskey, and those authorities didn't see anything in the law that contradicted what Maker's did.

Likewise, while I find Scotch enthusiasts tend to lean conservative in their tastes and their attitudes towards their favorite drink, bourbon lovers are often (admittedly, not always) more open to novel approaches and new whiskey makers. It's also my opinion that in Scotland, who does the innovation often matters more than what the innovation is. David Stewart got an MBE for his many contributions to Scotch whisky, among them bringing solera maturation and secondary barrel maturation into the industry. However, he was master blender at William Grant & Sons and a 50-year industry veteran, not a blender at a start-up founded by an American. In America, if a newcomer in Texas decides to make bourbon with an obscure strain of Aztec corn imported from Mexico, no one will stand in her way. Moreover, so long as it tastes good, most will celebrate it.

MAKER'S MARK'S
ONE-TIME NEIGHBORS

S tar Hill Farm and Maker's Mark lie in Marion County, smack in the geographic center of the state of Kentucky. It's also the historical center of Catholicism in the commonwealth, starting when a group of sixty Catholic families migrated from Maryland beginning in 1785. I have seen many different dates for when these Catholics founded the community of Holy Cross in what would become Marion County, but the first priest ordained in the United States, Father Stephen Badin, moved there in 1793.

Since the earliest days of the Union, Marion County was a Catholic island in what would become a sea of Protestants, and many of those Protestants took a dim view of alcohol. Kentucky has a long history of certain folks in rural counties not wanting liquor sold in their communities, while being more than happy to take a chunk of the taxes collected from the bourbon industry. Even today, alcohol sales remain restricted, at least to some degree, in all the counties along Marion's southern border.

As told by James Higdon in his book *The Cornbread Mafia*, Marion County's Catholic population was deeply embedded in the Kentucky bourbon industry, but generally viewed with suspicion by their neighbors. Prohibition put many Marion County residents out of work, and those unemployed distillery hands turned to moonshining and bootlegging. These strands of being a semi-ostracized community, friendly to inebriating substances, and an outlaw legacy all came together to give birth to a loose syndicate of pot farmers, one that began calling themselves the Cornbread Mafia in 1978. That syndicate was crushed by state and federal law enforcement a decade later.

By the time I began driving to Marion County to periodically visit Maker's Mark, the Cornbread Mafia was definitely over. Still, their legend persists to this day. The 1980s, when I was in high school, was a time of DEA agents and state police using small, single-engine planes to scout for crops of pot growing in isolated central Kentucky fields. Contrary to popular belief (one most recently referenced in the TV series *Justified*), those pot farms were never in the Appalachian Mountains, but instead were in what still is arguably the best stretch of land in America for growing marijuana. Most of the "Cornbreads" are out of prison now, released either due to ailing health or granted amnesty by President Obama. They held a reunion in Lebanon, the county seat, in April 2023.

Despite Maker's Mark's significant expansion, as well as the Limestone Branch Distillery and Diageo's touted carbon neutral distillery in Lebanon, Marion County still looks much the same to me as it did in the early 1990s. The part of the drive I continue to enjoy the most are the gleaming white front yard shrines, made of a concrete Mary statue installed in an apse fashioned from a half-buried bathtub. It remains the charming, bucolic, and thoroughly Catholic corner of Kentucky's bourbon country.

A NAME SYNONYMOUS WITH THE BOURBON WAREHOUSE AND THE BEST WHEATED BOURBON EVER

One of the physical features that separates Nelson County, Kentucky, and the hills of Lynchburg, Tennessee, from Speyside or the Province of Munster is the rickhouse. They might not be larger than the warehouses employed by some of their peers in terms of interior volume or storage capacity, but they do tower over them, with a typical rickhouse standing four or five stories high. Many are sided with metal sheeting, some with masonry, and certain modern rickhouses have a whole side clad in glass, so those driving by can see the stacks of barrels within. But it isn't the exterior of the building, but what those barrels are stacked inside that make the rickhouse different.

The design of the rickhouse was patented by Frederick Stitzel in 1879. To understand the advantages of Stitzel's design, one must know the limitations of the method it replaced: dunnage, meaning the barrels are laid on their side in a row and upon a pair of rails. Rows are stacked on top of each other, often three high. Dunnage has its advantages, foremost that it isn't infrastructure intensive, but a drawback is it puts enormous weight onto the casks of the bottom row, increasing the risk of failure for those bottom tier casks. Also, moving any cask on the bottom and middle tier (as might be necessary due to a leak or any number of other reasons) is laborious. Stitzel's rickhouse

design was engineered as a system of rows and columns of racks and enjoys three designed advantages over dunnage.

First, the structure supports the barrels, without depending on the strength of the barrels underneath. Next, one only needs to remove no more than a few barrels to access any barrel stored in the rickhouse. Finally, the design allows for multistory buildings, but without inhibiting the circulation of air between floors or around the individual barrels. If you simply put barrels in dunnage in a multistory warehouse, each floor becomes its own maturation space, wholly cut off from the others. The rickhouse design makes the entire warehouse an organic whole. To understand why, it is useful to think of the rickhouse as actually two separate structures: the ricks and the shell protecting the ricks from the weather.

Frederick Stitzel is sometimes accredited with originating wheated bourbon, but so is William Larue Weller. Those two names, Weller and Stitzel, became intertwined when Frederick's nephew Arthur opened the A. Ph. Stitzel Distillery in 1903, which became the source for W. L. Weller & Sons' whiskeys. The W. L. Weller & Sons company was bought by Julian Van Winkle in 1908, and Winkle, Weller, and Stitzel all weathered the dark days of Prohibition together with one of the six "medicinal" liquor licenses.

After the repeal of Prohibition, the distiller and the brand merged to form Stitzel-Weller, and they built a new distillery in Shively (an industrial suburb of Louisville) in 1935. Whether it was Weller or Stitzel who actually invented wheated bourbon, the distillery named for both of them made a wheated bourbon that became famous in modern times as pure ambrosia. The distillery was, sadly, shuttered in 1992, as part of the lingering fallout of the Great Whiskey Bust.

The flagship brand of Stitzel-Weller was Old Fitzgerald, and pre-1992 Old Fitzgerald is an ardently sought-after collectable today. The Old Fitzgerald brand continues in new production as a wheated bourbon made by Heaven Hill, while the Weller name lives on as a wheated line of bourbons made by Buffalo Trace. The Van Winkles lent their name to their own bourbon brand, initially building its reputation on stocks of excellent and quite old Stitzel-Weller bourbon. Finally, the rickhouses of the Stitzel-Weller Distillery continue in use today, and even if there are no plans to revive distilling there, it is the brand home for Blade & Bow.

LIVING LEGEND: JIMMY RUSSELL

Another one of those early encounters with Kentucky bourbondom that happened when I was sixteen didn't take on any significance for me until decades later. That was the year when a pair of Jack Russells on my father's horse farm produced a large litter of puppies, too large to retain on the farm. So, my sister and I joined our dad at the September horse sale at Keeneland, and that was where I met Jimmy Russell for the first time.

JIMMY RUSSELL AND HIS SON, EDDIE

I had no idea who he was, and I imagine neither did most everyone else at Keeneland that day, because this was the Kentucky of 1988. Another twenty years would pass before being a master distiller of a major bourbon distillery conferred rock star status. I didn't even get his name, and thus didn't pick up on the silly coincidence of trying to sell a Jack Russell to Jimmy Russell. I wouldn't realize who he was until I shook his hand again at the opening of the Wild Turkey Visitor Center in 2014.

Just because Russell was obscure at the time didn't mean he wasn't already doing the work that would make him a living legend, reviving the fortunes of the bourbon industry. Russell grew up just five miles from the Lawrenceburg, Kentucky, distillery. His own father was a distillery worker and, following his father's footsteps, began working at Wild Turkey in 1954. His apprenticeship making bourbon was under Bill Hughes and Ernest Ripy Jr. (the great-grandson of Wild Turkey's founder), the second and third master distillers there. By the time I first met him in 1988, Russell had already been master distiller at Wild Turkey for two decades, guiding it through the long slump years of the 1970s and 1980s.

Russell didn't step back from running Wild Turkey's distilling operations until 2015, so the modern identity of Wild Turkey bourbon is very much his creation. It's not for nothing that industry folks were calling him "the Buddha of Bourbon" decades ago. He played a major part in the Small Batch era of the 1990s that helped propel bourbon into revival, introducing Rare Breed in 1991 and Kentucky Spirit in 1994. Russell also consolidated a new dynasty in Kentucky bourbon, when his son Eddie became his successor in 2015.

Yet perhaps most important of all was that he was also one of those people who, like Booker Noe, took to the road, educating consumers in person and inventing the public relations role that is so much a part of the way we think of master distillers today. Also, like Booker Noe, Russell had one of those larger-than-life personalities, albeit more folksy than gregarious in his case. Although the revival of bourbon's fortunes was centered on pushing it as a premium product, Russell was not one for pretensions. In a move that would make many a snob wince, Russell kept his own stash of Rare Breed in a freezer. If the bourbon was already ice cold, Russell would say, he didn't need to add ice, which only dilutes the bourbon. Moreover, in those days he often drank his bourbon from a Dixie cup.

FOUR ROSES

When one drives over the train tracks crossing Bonds Mill Road and reaches Four Roses Distillery for the first time, the thought that comes to mind is that this place was built as a showplace for bourbon. I first came upon it in 1990, back when it was still obscure and known as the Old Prentice Distillery. At that time, nobody cared anything for the place and what it was doing, except the employees, some corporate overlords, and perhaps the Japanese.

The notion that it must have been designed as a showcase from the beginning is because of the gorgeous Mission Revival architecture of the stillhouse. With its red tile roofing and yellow stucco walls, the building makes a statement in the Bluegrass. At the time of my first encounter with the place, I was aware of just one other building in the whole state done in that style; I still don't need all my fingers to count the examples I know of today. The look of the distillery is so distinctive that it has become iconic among those tourists who have followed most or all of the Kentucky Bourbon Trail, even if they do not count themselves one of Four Roses' diehard fans.

Yet why Old Prentice was built in this way is a mystery. "I wish I knew," said Four Roses' master distiller Brent Elliott. "There is nothing about it in writing."

My own guess is that the distillery was indeed intended as a showplace, much as Old Taylor (now Castle & Key) was, and that the Mission Revival style was in vogue when the stillhouse was constructed in 1910. It's one of those gems of the Kentucky bourbon industry that enthusiasts and Kentuckians in general should be delighted survived the industry's bottoming out in the 1980s, helped no doubt by making the National Register of Historic Places in 1987. It could very well have been shuttered and fallen into ruins, which is exactly what happened to the aforementioned Old Taylor.

During the 20th century, Four Roses very much defied the odds. Before Prohibition and in the mid-20th century, Four Roses was a very well-regarded bourbon, with top sales numbers in the 1940s and '50s. But the brand and distillery were acquired by the burgeoning Canadian drinks giant Seagram in 1943, and in 1945 they decided to take advantage of the popularity of Four Roses Bourbon by introducing a cheaper blended whiskey to sell alongside it. That blend was mostly grain-neutral spirits (basically vodka). The Four Roses Blended Whiskey did well enough, but never as well as the bourbon.

That move was followed just a few years later by Seagram's decision to discontinue Four Roses Bourbon in the American market altogether. Nobody knows for certain why the conglomerate did this, but it's generally believed that Seagram CEO Samuel Bronfman wanted to clear market space for his Canadian brands, like Seagram 7 and Seagram VO, and imports like Dewar's. Regardless, Seagram employed an old trick in the whiskey business: cash in on a well-established brand by replacing it with a cheaper version, making minimal changes to the labeling, then crossing their fingers in hopes nobody notices. But consumers did notice, and sales of Four Roses slid precipitously. After decades of being associated with a bottom shelf product, Four Roses' reputation was in tatters by the time I had my first look around the distillery. None of the spirits that went into the blended whiskey were ever made at Old Prentice; the stuff was instead coming from other Seagram-owned plants, including the one in Lawrenceburg, Indiana (coincidentally, the same town name as Four Roses' home near Lawrenceburg, Kentucky), that is today known as MGP/the Ross & Squibb Distillery, where most of the aged stock whiskey used in making America's abundance of sourced brands comes from.

Yet, while Four Roses Bourbon was banished from the United States, it continued as an export product, and in that remnant

FOUR ROSES DISTILLERY

lay the root of the brand's revival. In particular, the bourbon held onto its strong reputation in Japan. That became important at the turn of the 20th century, because Seagram continued to suffer under the same Bronfman business sense that led it to degrade its own brands. By the 1990s, Jim Rutledge was master distiller at Old Prentice, and he was a tireless advocate for reinstituting the bourbon into the American market. His pleas fell on deaf ears. A story I've heard Rutledge tell is of how, after much agitation, he finally persuaded Seagram in 1996 to sell Four Roses Bourbon in Kentucky, so the Old Prentice employees could buy their handiwork without having to fly to Europe or Japan. His bosses relented and agreed to allow this, but rubbed salt into the matter by telling him that they wouldn't spend one red cent on building the brand. It was the capstone of five decades of Seagram not caring a jot for the Four Roses business.

While Four Roses was being grudgingly sold in Kentucky, Samuel Bronfman's successor and grandson, Edgar Bronfman Jr., took the conglomerate heavily into the entertainment industry, acquiring Universal Studios, MCA, PolyGram, and other companies. This misadventure led to the breakup of Seagram. Bronfman moved on from the collapse of his historic family company, as corporate aristocrats often do, to work in the corporate entertainment industry, becoming CEO and then chairman of Warner Music. The sell-off of corporate assets that followed was a foundational event in the international whiskey business as we know it today, and one part of it was how Japanese appreciation for Four Roses Bourbon came to fruition.

In December 2001, Kirin Brewing bought Four Roses. As Brent Elliott put it, "The Japanese threw us a lifeline." They began the next year by discontinuing the blended whiskey and reintroducing Four Roses Bourbon to the United States. As if to emphasize the change of direction, Kirin offered to buy back every bottle of the down-market Four Roses blended whiskey from distributors, clearing it from the marketplace so their rehabilitation of the brand's reputation could begin. No one would confuse the old, cheapie Seagram stuff with the genuine article as they began investing in building up the brand name anew.

The timing could not have been better, either, because the new ownership brought their determination for reinventing Four Roses to the table just a few years before the Bourbon Boom began picking up steam. Kirin's backing and Rutledge's commitment and vision were like a surfer perfectly positioned to catch the big breaker rolling in.

That rebirth was a quarter of a century ago. Since then, Rutledge has moved on to other ventures, and was succeeded by Brent Elliott in 2015, who is now a fixture among Kentucky's master distillers. Four Roses Bourbon has grown from one to four expressions in regular release, one for each blossom on the logo: the core bourbon, Small Batch, Small Batch Select, and Single Barrel. For many bourbon fans, the tales about when Four Roses was seen as rotgut are just stories, because it is so hard to imagine Kentucky bourbon without the good stuff coming out of that curious yellow Mission Revival stillhouse.

THE 10 RECIPES OF
FOUR ROSES

Part of why Four Roses attracts such a devoted fan base is that their method for making bourbon is like a kind of honey for whiskey nerd-dom. The distillery doesn't make just one or two types of bourbon, as many major Kentucky distilleries do. Instead, they make 10.

They start with two distinct mash bills, labeled B and E. The former is 60 percent corn, 35 percent rye, and 5 percent malted barley, and follows the spicy "high rye" style. The other recipe is in the traditional bourbon style, with a more typical level of rye content: 75 percent corn, 20 percent rye, and 5 percent malted barley.

So far, the Four Roses production process is much like those of their peers; having two or three bourbon mash bills is the norm among the big Kentucky distillers. The difference is that Four Roses regularly employs five distinct strains of yeast and applies each to the two mash bills. As is the case for baking, yeast matters as much as the grain in how a whiskey will come to taste in the end. By having five house strains of yeast and two mash bills, Four Roses produces 10 separate types of bourbon.

The yeast strains are labeled F, K, O, Q, and Y. The ten recipes are referred to in code, a quirky touch that bourbon nerds adore. An example is OBSK, which means the high rye bourbon made with the K yeast strain. This recipe combines the high rye grain bill with their yeast known for producing spicy, robust flavors, doubling down on the idea of producing a spicy, rather than a sweet, bourbon. Of the other four, V is noted for producing delicate fruit notes; O creates a richer fruit experience; Q is floral; and F is herbal.

Four Roses uses these 10 recipes like colors on a blender's palette, and while they are encountered individually only in single barrel bottlings, one version uses all ten—Four Roses Bourbon (popularly referred to as "Yellow Label"). "Center mass for our products is on the Ks and Vs," says Brent Elliott, "and any special edition ever will have one or the other, but not both." The other yeast and grain combinations are treated as flavoring elements, tweaking the choice of foundational bourbon. So, Four Roses Small Batch is made using OBSK, OBSO, OESK, and OESO.

The 10-recipe system is a legacy of the Seagram era, when the distillery was making Four Roses Bourbon for export, but also whiskeys to feed other requirements for the parent corporation. That raises the question of why Seagram wanted a high rye bourbon, as opposed to a wheated or high corn variety. "My guess is that Seagram was a Canadian company," says Elliott, "and Canadian whisky is rye-based."

The idea of building on the legacy with another recipe has been mused upon at Four Roses for many years, but until recently musing was all it came to. "We haven't had the capacity to do it," says Elliott. "Since I've been here, we've had problems just meeting demand." But since Four Roses completed its

expansion project in 2019, doubling their output, they've managed to carve out a little breathing space, and the idea of trying something new is being visited more seriously these days. "Something will happen. I just don't know what or when yet."

FOUR ROSES' OTHER IDIOSYNCRATIC BUILDINGS

Another feature that makes Four Roses unique among Kentucky distillers isn't found at the Lawrenceburg distillery. The company makes its bourbon and puts it into barrels in Lawrenceburg, but those barrels then go onto trucks for shipping down to their Bardstown property, Cox's Creek, where it is aged, dumped, and bottled. It is where those barrels are aged that is so peculiar, because Four Roses is the only major distiller in Kentucky to rely on one-story warehouses.

Driving along the byways of the Bluegrass, the most common sight after horses and barns are bourbon warehouses. These are often unmistakable and mammoth structures, four to six stories tall, that dominate the surrounding countryside. But what one finds at Cox's Creek is more akin to the dunnage warehouses of Scotland. Sometimes called "low houses," these grey buildings are just tall enough to store six ricks of barrels.

When these curious low houses come up in talks with enthusiasts and even other writers, the two most common explanations

I hear are "I don't know" and "they did it that way because it's cheaper to build." I didn't need to even ask Four Roses to know the latter explanation is wrong. My experience in the building industry tells me the construction footprint for those buildings is already so expensive that it wouldn't be economical to rely on a series of single-story buildings in the way Four Roses does without a compelling reason. That reason, it turns out, really is about cutting costs, but the cost they had in mind had nothing to do with construction.

Brent Elliot explained it to me like this: "From everything I've heard, it was all about consistency. Those were built back when barrel rotation was much more common." Nowadays, the practice of pulling the barrels from the ricks and moving them around to achieve consistent maturation is a signature of Maker's Mark, but no one else in Kentucky employs it. The reason that is necessary is because of the thermodynamic properties of the buildings in question: it gets toasty on

the upper floors, which speeds evaporation and certain other parts of the maturation process, while what takes place on the ground floor is slower, gentler, and involves less frequent visits by thirsty angels. If a bourbon maker wants all their barrels to come out more or less the same, they can do one of two things: move the barrels around periodically or put them in a single-story warehouse, and moving the barrels is labor intensive.

As it is often said, maturation contributes at least half to how any whiskey turns out, so those low houses are integral to the Four Roses identity. The company announced in 2023 that it would build 17 more of them, adding 776,000 square feet of warehousing space.

Another idiosyncratic, cost-saving feature of Cox's Creek is now sadly a thing of the past. The property once also doubled as a cattle farm. In a now bygone time, Four Roses allowed cattle to graze on the property. They collected a modest fee, and it saved on mowing costs. One can also imagine it added to the bucolic charm of the place, but it had the downside of leaving the property dotted with cow patties. As bourbon tourism became popular, especially around Bardstown, the management decided it was worth the mowing fees if that meant not having the visitors stumble into a wet cow patty.

THE FORGOTTEN BACKGROUND TO KIRIN'S LOVE OF FOUR ROSES

The Japanese appreciation for Four Roses bourbon, as well as the connection between Kirin Brewing and Four Roses Distillery, are manifest in more ways than the 2002 purchase of the distillery and brand by the Japanese drinks company. Those ties between Kirin and Kentucky bourbon are rooted in Kirin's first entry into making whisky, the Fuji Gotemba Distillery.

In 1973, Kirin got into the Japanese whisky business and opened their own distillery, Fuji Gotemba, but initially they were not pursuing it as a solo enterprise. The construction of Fuji Gotemba began as the project of an international consortium consisting of Kirin, Chivas Brothers, and Seagram. At the time, the Four Roses brand and the Old Prentice Distillery in Lawrenceburg, Kentucky, were both owned by Seagram.

The distillery has a number of special features attached to it. For example, it is one of just a handful of distilleries in the world making both malt and grain whiskies in the same plant. By some measures—namely square footage and excluding those whiskey-making facilities not using the Scotch model— it is the largest whisky distillery in the world. The property also lies at the base of the famous Mt. Fuji.

Fuji Gotemba's most interesting technical distinction, however, is one that ties it back to that connection with Seagram and

Four Roses: the distillery uses a column still with a doubler setup. The original Coffey still design used two columns, an analyzer column, and a rectifier column, but there are many variants on that system. The grain whisky stills at Girvan in Scotland look more like they belong at an oil refinery than a drinks maker, and vodka distillers might have four or even five columns in a system. For its part, Fuji Gotemba has an American style column still.

A doubler is basically a pot still attached to a column still and finishes the distillation process. The American column still employs one column for the first round of distillation, then feeds those low wines (low strength spirit) into a doubler, not another column. A similar mechanism is called a thumper, and the only important distinction between a thumper and a doubler is how that pot is heated. This is an almost uniquely American design, and that "almost" hinges on Fuji Gotemba, as it is the only distillery outside of the US to use a doubler.

The result of this peculiar engineering choice is that Fuji Gotemba's grain whisky new make is heavier than its peers, either in Japan, Scotland, or Ireland. One could say it is an almost bourbon-like grain whisky, in fact. It has never been confirmed that this oddity is a result of the participation of Four Roses owner Seagram in the distillery construction, but that is the logical guess.

Another influence Four Roses has on Kirin's original whisky-making venture is in its maturation. As Japanese whisky is based on Scottish techniques, they are (like the Scots) heavily reliant on used casks to age their whiskies. Kirin owns their own bourbon distillery, so for twenty years their Japanese whiskies have been drawing on ex-Four Roses barrels as their primary cask stock.

LOVE OR IP THEFT?

T he story of how Four Roses got started, and how it came to be adorned with the quadruple rose logo, is as much of a tall tale as any whiskey story to be heard. In 1884, Paul Jones Jr. moved his grocery business from Atlanta to 118 East Main Street in Louisville, Kentucky. That move makes more sense in the context of the time, seeing as how when Jones moved, it was only 20 years after General Sherman's bluecoats had razed much of Atlanta. In the 19th century, grocers starting whiskey companies was par for the course; Johnnie Walker and Nelson's Greenbrier have similar origin stories, just to name two. So, Jones may have been involved in trading whiskey before moving to Louisville, which would have given him additional incentive to move there and may also explain his claim to have been making Four Roses since the 1860s. Regardless, he didn't trademark the brand until 1888.

He chose Four Roses because of a woman, or so the story goes. Jones claimed he was head over heels for a beautiful belle, and proposed marriage. In keeping with the Victorian era's practice of passing signals with flowers, if this unnamed belle answered yes, she would wear a corsage of roses on her dress at a ball they both would be attending. She came and was wearing a corsage of four red roses.

This story is the official version, and if it is true, it has a bittersweet ending. If that belle was ever real, she rejected Jones's claim in the end, because he died a bachelor. His nephew Lawrence took over the company after his 1895 passing.

But there is another version of how the brand got its name. After the Civil War, a Union veteran and doctor named Rufus Rose moved to Atlanta and got into the distilling business. Rufus bottled his whiskey in clay jugs bearing the distillery logo, four roses, representing his four daughters. Another version says the four roses were Rufus, his brother Origen, and their sons. You can still see the house Rose built with his success, a Victorian mansion on Peachtree Street.

However, Rose didn't sell the business to Jones, despite the gaining power of the temperance movement in Georgia. Instead, they moved it to Chattanooga, Tennessee, after Georgia enacted full Prohibition in 1907. So perhaps Jones was inspired by Rose, but the Four Roses started by Jones isn't the same as what was sold by the R. M. Rose Company.

How things came to bear this name or look the way they do is often hazy in the whiskey business. In a more modern example of how this works at Four Roses, the reverse pear shape of the Four Roses Small Batch bottle is often said to be expressly designed to be reminiscent of a closed rose bud. The only problem with that is folks at the distillery don't know whether that is true and swear nothing was ever written down about it. Brent Elliott has told me that among those who were there at the time, this claim produces head scratching and confused questions of "Is that what we meant to do?"

So, perhaps Jones was inspired by Rose. Or maybe he was inspired by a Southern belle. Or maybe he just really liked flowers. As with so much else about bourbon in the 19th century, we will probably never know for sure, but the Four Roses of today likes the belle version of events.

LET THE BOOM TIMES ROLL?

Although plenty of money has been made in the world's whiskey industries, taken as a whole, the 20th century was a terrible time to be doing business in it. Some calamities were felt evenly, while others were particular to a region. When I look at the timeline, it's hard to find a stretch of good times for any part of the industry that lasted so much as a generation. Instability, downturn, or worse were the norm.

In the early 20th century, the rising temperance movement was nibbling away at whiskey makers in America. Tennessee introduced statewide Prohibition in 1909, chasing its distilling companies to other states until they were shut down there, too, either by that state going dry or by national Prohibition becoming the law with the ratification of the 18th Amendment in 1919. But often overlooked is that Canada saw one province after another enact its own Prohibition, so that by 1917 the sale of alcohol was banned over most of the country. The exception was Quebec, where an alcohol ban lasted only a few months in 1919. Most provinces repealed their temperance measures during the 1920s, but Canada's most populous province of Ontario waited until 1927 to relegalize drinking. Prince Edward Island wouldn't reverse their ban until 1948.

During these pre-Prohibition years, distillers in Scotland and Ireland were largely safe from political and legal harassment by temperance forces, but they were subject to restrictions as part of World War I era food rationing. Those restrictions have had a lasting impact on Irish and Scotch whiskies to this day. The legal minimum strength of whisky in Great Britain was 43 percent until 1916, when it was cut to 40 percent as a grain-saving measure, and 40 percent has remained the minimum for almost the entire world ever since.

While the damage done by Prohibition was most vicious in the United States, the pain was felt in Ireland and Scotland, as well. In America many distilling companies closed and never returned. With production shut down well into the 1930s, inventories of maturing whiskey wouldn't be rebuilt in a general sense until the eve of World War II. Yet it shouldn't be forgotten that the Irish, Scots, and Canadians relied heavily on the United States as an export market. Then and now, the US is the world's most lucrative market for whiskey sales, and losing that market hurt all the other industries. Bootlegging could never make up for the volume of legal trade, and they all suffered cutbacks and closures as a result.

Before Prohibition could be repealed in December 1933, the Wall Street Crash of 1929 had already ushered in the Great Depression. Although how hard the Depression bit depended on what country you lived in, nowhere and no one avoided the withering effects of global economic collapse. Making things even worse for the Irish was the beginning of the Anglo-Irish Trade War, starting in 1932. Just as the American market reopened, the Irish were shut out from the markets of both Britain and its empire. The Irish whiskey industry was devastated.

The Second World War brought with it renewed rationing, and this time it affected American producers as well. American distillers faced not just restrictions on using grain to make whiskey, but also on access to oak for making barrels. It was during this time that the American Standard Barrel shifted from 48 gallons to the current 53 gallons, a change calculated to make the most use of what wood was available while still fitting into the existing rickhouse infrastructure. In Scotland, whisky distilling was banned from 1940 to 1944, with the result that the entire output of Scotland during the war years was approximately equal to the output of the nine pre-war months of 1939. Wartime rationing in Britain continued until well after the war, and grain restrictions on the Scotch industry weren't fully lifted until 1954.

The only whisky industry that truly prospered during the Depression and the Second World War was that of Japan, which furnished vast quantities of spirits to the Imperial Army and Navy from the late 1930s to the end of the war. Quite the opposite from the experience of other national industries, Japanese whisky makers received priority access to commodities like barley. Yoichi Distillery was designated as a naval installation, for example. The war years were a golden age for Japanese whisky, at least until American bombing obliterated Japanese infrastructure.

Just as Britain was weighed down by continued wartime restrictions until the middle 1950s, the American whiskey industry was also hampered by the Korean War. Some leaders in the business, particularly Louis Rosenstiel of Schenley Industries, believed the Korean War would become another world war. Hoping to get ahead of the restrictions another total war would bring, Rosenstiel decided to ramp up production while he still could, to forestall what he thought would be future shortage. Schenley was one of the Big Four of the business in North America, and his vast overproduction had ripple effects for the entire bourbon business well into the 1960s, pushing prices down and forcing some producers out of business. This is what prompted the closure of the James E. Pepper Distillery, a Schenley property, located not even a mile from my house, in 1958.

The final injury suffered by the world's whiskey industries in the 20th century came in the 1970s. The economic situation for Canada, Ireland, the UK, and the US were all dismal for much of that decade, with only Japan prospering. The hard times coincided with a period when the tastes of younger drinkers were shifting away from whiskey and towards other drinks, such as wine. The result was the Great Whiskey Bust, a slump that had far-reaching repercussions that are spelled out in many of the tales told in this book.

The years since the 1990s have generally been good ones for whiskey makers around the world. Their challenges have been meeting surging demand, not surviving during a years-long stoppage or finding a way to offload surplus supply and eke out a profit on it. If this account demonstrates anything, it is just how magical the recent thirty years of good times are relative to historical experience, and that is why one often hears industry professionals murmur about just when and how the boom will come to an end.

WHISKEY COWS

Many of the experiences that sparked my curiosity about whiskey came in my 16th year. I described exploring Glenn's Creek earlier, but another, lesser experience was my first encounter with "whiskey cows." My father had leased some unused pasturage to a local cattle farmer, and one day while I was mending and painting a fence, that farmer showed up with his pickup. Instead of a bed, there was a very improvised-looking tanker in the back. From a spigot out the back of that tanker, he filled a row of troughs with what at the time was a very odd smelling slop, and then admitted his herd through a gate to slurp it up.

That odd smell would become very familiar later in life, because it was stillage, or the leftovers of cooking, fermenting, and distilling grain. In recent years, many a story has been spun about how feeding these leftovers to livestock is a modern, eco-friendly innovation, but it's really as old as the farmer-distiller of yesteryear. For an 18th-century farmer-distiller, turning some of his grain into whiskey for sale, and then feeding the spent grain back to his cattle or pigs, was rugged efficiency. For a commercial distillery, it's the solution to a major disposal problem.

When a distiller goes to work on grain, what they want is to turn the grain's starch into sugar, and then into alcohol for extraction. But grain also has protein and fat content, and the fat and protein content in distiller's grains is often higher than in regular feed grain. A big distillery will give this stuff away for free to any farmer who comes and gets it, because they produce it in huge amounts.

In Kentucky, for every gallon of bourbon a distillation run produces, approximately ten gallons of stillage is left behind. Jack Daniel's Distillery typically produces 500,000 gallons of slop per day, a vast amount of byproduct. If nobody comes to get any for two or three days, it is not unheard of to have a major distillery shut down production due to the storage and disposal issues. Many of the large distilleries in Kentucky and Tennessee have even installed equipment for drying out the stillage into solid, spent grains, to make it even more attractive to the cattle farmers. Slop will spoil after two to three days in summer, and freeze in winter, but the dry, spent grain has a longer shelf life.

This practice of feeding spent whiskey grain to livestock isn't merely a Kentucky or Tennessee thing. The famed Wagyu cattle of Japan are fed, in part, on spent grains from the Japanese distilling and brewing industries. Cattle in Ireland, Scotland, and Canada are also fed spent grains. Many American craft distillers also supply stillage to local livestock farmers, but this isn't always possible, especially for urban distilleries. "Whiskey cows" are far from some novel, green innovation, with the practice of feeding pigs and cows spent grain being almost as universal as it is time-tested.

Yet the modern world whiskey boom has put a wrinkle into that practice. Some distilleries are now producing so much grain that local and even regional agriculture can no longer consume their output. Jack Daniel's is addressing their huge output in partnership with 3 Rivers Energy by building a bio-gas digester. The distillery will continue to offer stillage to local farmers, but approximately two-thirds of their stillage will go to the new bio-gas plant. The plant's output will meet most of the distillery's gas demand while also reducing their energy demands, as they will no longer need to dry as much stillage for the sake of making it more attractive animal feed.

Jack Daniel's isn't alone in this new use for stillage. Yoichi Distillery opened a bio-gas and electric plant in 2020, so they not only turn their stillage into gas, but use the gas to generate electricity.

SCOTCH MEANS MANY THINGS

In most respects, the Scotch whisky narrative is much like that of its peers, even those in America and Canada. I find it remarkable how similar, for example, the stories of a Colonel Taylor, James Pepper, or George Garvin Brown (in their broad strokes) are to that of an Alexander Walker, Tommy Dewar, or William Grant. These characters were all of the same era, Big Bourbon and Big Scotch were taking shape at much the same time, and that shaping was mostly done by the same kinds of people: businessmen, not distillers or blenders. That isn't how many folks like to think of it, that they owe their favorite tipple to a marketeer rather than a craftsman, but that is the general truth of it.

Yet Scotland, like every major whisky-making nation, has a slate of characteristics that make its whisky unique, and one in particular impacts their stories and how they are told. I'm thinking of Scotland's long-established breadth of malt whisky making. The craft spirits boom in the United States had expanded the number of active whiskey-making distilleries to over 750 by the end of 2022, but just twenty years before, there were fewer than twenty nationwide. By contrast, the 1976 *New York Times* article "Dark Days for Scotland's Own" declared the previous year had been the worst on record for the Scotch business. It was written in the midst of the Great Whiskey Bust, and yet it stated there were 126 active distilleries in Scotland at the time. The closures prompted by the Bust never shrank that number below several dozen, and at the time I am writing, the count is set to pass 150 in either 2024 or 2025.

That is a lot of medium and large distilleries at work because none operate at the microdistillery level. All have their own particular identity and most have a history stretching back a century or longer. A collection of just the ghost stories associated with all those places could fill a book on their own. Malt distilleries are the heart of the Scotch industry, but they are not its backbone, which is instead found in its blended whiskies. Most of Scotland's malt distilleries were founded for the express purpose of feeding malt whisky to those blended whiskies and didn't find strong identities of their own as single malts until modern times.

That matters in the mythology of Scotch, because although there are some recognized malt names in the story of the Pattinson Whisky Crash (see page 205), they weren't trying to swindle investors on the backs of The Glenfarclas. They were doing it by employing a business model geared around brands of blended whiskies. Likewise, if Johnnie Walker Red and Black are said to contain up to forty distinct whiskies in their blends, the individual constituents might be vital to the whisky in the bottle, but their individual stories don't matter a jot to the larger story of Johnnie Walker.

My belief is the commercial weight of the big blends and the sheer plethora of individual malt distilleries have shifted the spotlight away to an extent. For example, Strathisla is the oldest of the active distilleries in Scotland, dating back to 1786, in the pre-legalization era. But when I visited there in 2017, the

tour gave that point equal weight with the distillery's pagoda architecture and the construction of the washback. There was none of the mythology that Bushmills, for example, attaches to its claim of being the oldest licensed whiskey distillery there is. It was technical accounting more than a bard's crafting.

Yet one can't have whiskey without distilleries. In Scotland, the profusion is organized into five distinct regions, as recognized by the Scotch Whisky Association (SWA): Campbeltown, Highland, Islay, Lowland, and Speyside. Some experts disagree with that interpretation, but the SWA is the industry's official voice on the matter. To give a hint of what is out there, it's necessary to address at least one example from each region.

CAMPBELTOWN: SPRINGBANK

As a region, Campbeltown was hard hit by the Great Whisky Bust. At one time, the peninsula was home to over thirty working distilleries, but now there are just three. Springbank is the oldest of the survivors, dating to 1828. But Springbank's long history is a classic example of another problem besetting storytelling from the point of view of a malt whisky distillery: it is so much like all the others. The plant was badly damaged in a storm in 1883, and again in 1902. It was shuttered in 1926 due to Prohibition and again in 1979 due to the UK's economic slump and the industry's own declining sales. During that time, ownership of the distillery changed hands multiple times.

But Springbank uses its output of both peated and unpeated malt with the many types of casks to produce three single malt brands all its own: Longrow, Hazelburn, and Springbank. They are also the only distillery in Scotland that manages the entirety of the production process on site, the two key particulars being they malt all their own barley (most other distilleries with malting floors rely on at least some subcontracted malt to meet requirements) and they mature all their whisky on their own property.

HIGHLAND: SCAPA

Scapa is located on Orkney, the main island in a chain of remote northern isles of the same name, so remote that they remained Viking property until 1468. One gripping yarn about Scapa is from the end of World War I. As has already been explored, fire is the enemy of anyone in the distilling business, and Scapa almost burnt to the ground in 1919. It was saved only because Scapa also happens to be a major base of the Royal Navy (the ships are moored in Scapa Flow), used extensively in World War I and II. The sailors of the post-war remnants of the Grand Fleet formed a bucket brigade, hauling seawater up to douse the blaze, a few gallons at a time.

Today you will see seals rather than battleships on the water, but Scapa still has its curiosities, foremost among them its Lomond still. A precursor to the modern hybrid still, the Lomond was invented in 1955 and features three perforated plates inserted into its neck. The plates are designed to allow adjustable control of the reflux, and when I was at Scapa they told me they had been removed. So, it's a rare piece of technology: Bruichladdich has one, salvaged from the defunct Inverleven, and Loch Lomond has two. Those are the only legacy examples in all of Scotland, and only a couple more contemporary examples have been built for new distilleries since.

HIGHLAND: BRORA

Brora is the singular example of how closing a distillery can turn it into a cult obsession in spite of the distillery's larger history. Brora's origins are tainted by its association with the infamous Sutherland Clearances. The distillery was constructed in 1819 (before the licensing reform in 1823), towards the end of a 12-year campaign of forced evictions of some 15,000 farmers from the lands of the Marquis of Stafford (later Duke of Sutherland) and his wife. This brutal, ugly affair was instigated largely by the Countess Stafford, who wished to replace the unprofitable tenant farmers with more lucrative ventures, mostly sheep grazing. A majority of the dispossessed immigrated to Australia or Canada, but some were put to work in the various business ventures that displaced them, and one of those ventures was Brora.

Another wrinkle is that when it was founded, Brora was known as Clynelish. In the late 1960s, the ownership of the time needed to expand production, but it was determined that building a second distillery would be more efficient than expanding the original. So, Clynelish 2 grew up next door. Then in 1975, the government banned two distilleries from having the same name. The original Clynelish, already running at reduced capacity, became Brora.

Brora closed in 1983. The lightly peated Highland malt available in bottlings nowadays was made in the 1970s and early

1980s, so it is all over 40 years old. The current owner, Diageo, finally reopened production at Brora in 2021, and youngish Brora could appear on the market by the end of the 2020s, although sometime in the 2030s is more likely.

ISLAY: LAPHROAIG

Founded in 1815 by Donald and Alexander Johnston of Clan Donald, Laphroaig is one of the whiskies that make Islay so famously smoky. The distillery stayed in the family until 1954, with the passing of Ian Hunter (who was nephew of Sandy Johnston; recall Booker Noe is a grandson of James B. Beam, despite the last name).

Laphroaig received its royal warrant in 1994, essentially a designation as an official supplier to the royal family. There have been many whiskies to receive such a warrant over the decades, but what makes Laphroaig's special is that it came from the then-Prince of Wales, that being the only warrant he has ever given to a whisky. Laphroaig 15 Year Old (a discontinued expression) is the favorite whisky of King Charles III, and it's said he never travels without bringing a bottle.

LOWLAND: GIRVAN

The Lowlands are another region that was hard hit by closures, so much so that the number of single malt bottlings based on stocks leftover from shuttered distilleries (Rosebank, Kinclaith, Interleven, Ladyburn, etc.) outnumber the legacy distilleries still in operation. Yet this most southerly region of Scotland has seen a rebound in recent years, with several new distilleries opened or under construction.

Girvan is the grain whisky distillery for William Grant & Sons, and thus instrumental in making their bread and butter blends like Grant's and Clan MacGregor. Grain distilleries like this one are often overlooked by even the most ardent enthusiasts, but that has begun changing, as grain whiskies are perfectly drinkable in their own right. Single grain whiskies have become a thing, and Girvan single grain expressions started appearing in 2014.

William Grant & Sons got into the grain whisky business in 1963, after a dispute between Charles Grant Gordon and their principal supplier. The plant was converted from a shuttered World War II munitions factory. Girvan has a long history of having other spirits either made there or having their production bolted onto it. Ladyburn malt was made there between 1966 and 1975, and Ailsa Bay was added to the complex in 2007. Some wags, apparently forgetting Ladyburn, took to calling Ailsa Bay "that shed in Girvan." Hendrick's Gin is also made at Girvan, and for many years was produced using the same equipment as the grain whisky.

SPEYSIDE: THE MACALLAN

The Highlands are the largest whisky region in terms of territory, but Speyside is where the majority of the industry's distilleries are located. If you want to spend weeks exploring Scotch whisky in person (and it will take you literal weeks), start by going to Aberdeen and renting a car. All of Speyside is in the vicinity.

The Macallan is arguably the most famous of the distilleries of Speyside nowadays. Even though it often occupies the third-place slot by volume of sales (behind The Glenfiddich and The Glenlivet), its whiskies command much higher prices than either. Any recent list of the most expensive whiskies in the world is topped by The Macallan plus some bottlings from Japan. At auction, Macallan bottlings have a tendency to elbow their way back into the top slot again and again.

Although they were marketing themselves as a malt whisky even before The Glenfiddich made its big push in the 1960s, they weren't nearly as famous as now, with their bottlings labeled as "The Macallan-Glenlivet." But by the 1970s, they had a strong reputation in their own right, and in the 1980s one began to see what would become a calling card of The Macallan: aggressively marketed, ultra-aged single malts. In 1983, they released an anniversary bottling labeled as a 50 year old (but was in fact at least 55 years old) in a limited run of just 500 bottles. Making expressions like that became a habit for The Macallan.

This prestige makes The Macallan a natural object for con jobs, including one of the most infamous in history. Famed

Chinese writer Zhang Wei took his grandmother on vacation in Switzerland, and decided to treat them both to a very heavy splurge at the Hotel Waldhaus am See: a pour of The Macallan 1878 priced at approximately $10,000. Wei posted about his splurge online, which prompted many questions and led the hotel (which thought it was in possession of a genuine item) to send a sample for verification. In 2017, carbon dating proved beyond a shadow of a doubt that it was a blended whisky (not even a single malt!) from the 1970s.

SPEYSIDE: AULTMORE

Built outside Keith in 1896 by Alexander Edward, the founder of so many Speyside distilleries, the Aultmore's stills are dumpy and run slowly, a combination that maximizes reflux. The malt whisky that comes out from this is noted for its heavier character and intensity, but that isn't why I am devoting some time to Aultmore. Instead, I list it because Aultmore's story underlines how blended whisky is the heart of the Scotch industry. This quite industrial-looking distillery didn't have a branded single malt of its own until 2015, with earlier bottlings of Aultmore coming from casks acquired by Scotland's thriving sector of negociants undertaking independent bottlings. It's said that if you want to try a pour of Aultmore malt around Keith, you don't mention it by name, but instead ask for "a dram of the Buckie Road."

Aultmore is one of those distilleries whose existence is still devoted to making blends. The distillery was acquired by John Dewar & Sons in 1923 and has been a key constituent in Dewar's blends ever since. This is so much the case that when

Bacardi was negotiating with Diageo over the acquisition of the Dewar's brand, Diageo is said to have wanted to keep Aultmore in their own portfolio. Bacardi threatened to walk away from the deal if they couldn't get the distillery in the package.

SPEYSIDE: CARDHU

Cardhu is one of the oldest distilleries in Speyside, but like so many making that claim, it traces its roots back to pre-1823 moonshiners John and Helen Cumming. Indeed, John Cumming was convicted of distilling without a license in 1816, leaving the operation of their Cardow Farm and illicit whisky business to his wife, Helen, for a time. They went legal in 1824, one of the early licensees coming out of the 1823 Excise Act.

By 1893, Cardow had become the key Highland malt being used in the blends at John Walker & Sons, so they made it their first distillery acquisition. Outside of the whisky's role in making Johnnie Walker, its esteem in vatted malts (a blend of malt whiskies with no grain whisky) and as a single malt led to the distillery being renamed in 1981 after the brand it spawned, from Cardow to Cardhu.

ROTTEN MOSS MAKES YOUR WHISKY TASTE GOOD (OR NOT)

As the source of the smoky flavor that characterizes so many Scotch whiskies, peat is whisky's most divisive ingredient. Whenever I ask people who like bourbon or Irish whiskey why they don't like Scotch, smoke is by far the most often cited cause. Peat is off-putting for some, but adored by others, and not all peat is created equal by mother nature.

Peat is decayed vegetable matter, submerged and compressed in a bog. The low oxygen content and high acidity of the stagnant water one finds in a bog greatly slows the decomposition of the rotting vegetation. The mosses that often contribute to the formation of peat also secrete tannins, which is why the streams running out of moors are so often brown in color, and tannins are natural preservatives. So, imagine a bunch of leaves, twigs, moss, grass clippings, and whatever else one might stuff in the compost bin or yard waste curbie, soaked, compressed, and left to rot ever so slowly over the course of not years, but millennia. Peat is the first step in the formation of coal, so it is useful to think of it as proto-coal.

Some regions of the world don't have wood as a reliable fuel source, such as parts of Scotland. In desert regions it's not uncommon to see people burn dried animal dung for fuel, but in wet, northerly places like Scotland, people were digging up peat, cutting it into blocks, and leaving it out to dry to use as fuel since prehistoric times. It comes into whisky making as a traditional fuel source. It's unlikely that the malt makers actually sought to impart a smoky flavor to their products, at least initially. They just needed a heat source for malting.

Peat and peated whiskies are a fixture of all parts of Scotland but are especially associated with the island of Islay (pronounced eye-la), home to just 3,000 people but nine distilleries. Peated whiskies are the signature style of the island, so much so that the unpeated whiskies made by Bruichladdich and especially Bunnahabhain are seen by many an enthusiast as curiosities, and by a few as heresies. Bunnahabhain doesn't make any peated whiskies, while Bruichladdich keeps a foot in by making Octomore, (in)famous as the most heavily peated whisky around.

Being a natural, organic feature, peat is localized in its character. Just within Scotland, there are noticeable differences in the composition and thus the smoky flavor of the peat. Mainland peat has more woody stem material, but less sphagnum moss going into it, when compared to the island peats. The mainland peat is better as a heat source but produces less of the smoky aromas that give Islay its identity.

These differences become even more profound once expanded to include peats from other parts of the globe, made up of their own distinctive basket of plants. Distillers in Washington State began experimenting with their native peat from the Skagit Valley before 2020. Matt Hoffman, master distiller at Westland Distillery, points to the presence of Labrador tea, cedar and fir needles, bog cranberry, and more in the peat as giving it an especially distinctive character. I've found the

Skagit peated malts from Copperworks and Westland have a more floral, less iodine character than their Islay counterparts.

Peat is not really a renewable resource; the bogs regenerate peat at the average rate of merely 1 mm per year. Although it sometimes seems like Islay is made out of peat, and sources across the Scotch industry insist they've got resources sufficient to last for centuries, rumors of Scotland running out of peat have percolated since before I started writing about whiskey. But even the 2023 news that Port Ellen Maltings, the only commercial malt maker on Islay, was restricting its sales wasn't actually about running out of peat. Instead, it was about a Scotland-wide problem of malting companies reaching the maximum output of their existing equipment, and that not being enough to meet demand. Every time I see a story about Scotland running out of peat, the real story seems to be that the article is just yellow journalism.

HOW A TAX BILL PAVED THE WAY FOR SCOTCH WHISKY

Scotch whisky enthusiasts and industry pros alike love to boast about its antique origins. On the Scotch Whisky Association website, the industry's trade group, one can read about the earliest written reference to whisky, a 1494 entry on the Exchequer Rolls: "Eight bolls of malt to Friar John Cor wherewith to make aqua vitae."

The thing about that line, though, is how much it underscores that the liquor wasn't anything like what we think of as Scotch whisky today. Aqua vitae, uisge beatha, call it what you will, but today we would call all that stuff new make or moonshine.

We can be certain of that because the first tax on whisky in Scotland was passed in 1644, with successive laws added after the union of Scotland and England in 1707. For much of the 18th century, licensing and taxes for whisky were a confused, expensive tangle, and few in Scotland bothered with legal production.

So, any story about a Scottish distillery tracing its origins back to the time of the Stuart kings is ultimately about a moonshining operation. Scotland's most famous poet, Robert Burns, worked for a time as what Americans would call a "revenuer," or booze taxman. By the early 19th century, thousands of stills were being seized every year. The Glenlivet that King George IV was purportedly quite fond of was being produced illegally at the time.

All that changed with the passage of a new British tax law, the Excise Act of 1823. This set the fee for a distiller's license at £10, plus a tax per gallon of proof spirit. To put that into perspective, the 1823 licensing fee is £1,600 ($2,000) in today's money, while the state and federal fees a new craft distiller in the US needs to pay to get licensed typically amounts to $5,000. Being a legal distiller in Scotland became affordable, and thus running a distilling business on the up-and-up became viable. Many Scottish moonshiners went legal, and in becoming legal, the door was opened for the

Scots' national drink to become the Scotch whisky industry as we know it today.

Other developments that came later, such as the invention of the Coffey still and the ability to export throughout the British Empire, were just as crucial, but I look at the Excise Act of 1823 as being the foundation for one crucial reason: it made aging Scotch whisky a safe and reliable business proposition. I'm sure the whiskies owned by kings and magnates managed to sit around in a cellar, aging in a cask, for long enough to become a recognizable single malt by today's standards. Yet for the most part, the business of making malt whisky in Scotland followed the same logic of moonshining everywhere: you don't lay up hundreds of gallons of your product for years and hope the exciseman won't find it and confiscate it. In Stuart or Georgian times, most Scottish whisky was white whisky, plain and simple, just like it was on the other side of the Atlantic. Written recipes for drinking the whisky of the 15th to 18th centuries read like a modern guide to making moonshine more palatable or how to do trendy white whiskey cocktails.

This is why I don't think of the Scotch whisky industry (or the Irish industry, for that matter) as being any older than its North American peers. The early Canadian and American distillers were often Scottish, Irish, or Welsh, and thus trace their know-how back to the same late medieval origins. Most importantly, the drinks in question only became recognizable to us moderns in the early 19th century, because that is when the proper suite of technology came into existence and production processes became formalized.

THE PATTINSON
WHISKY CRASH

The early 20th century saw a crash in the Scotch whisky industry, but unlike the Great Whiskey Bust of the 1970s, it had nothing to do with declining sales and changing tastes. Whisky was popular and remained so for decades after. Instead, the Pattinson Crash was more akin to the Enron or FTX scandals.

Driven by the entrepreneurial zeal of firms like John Dewar & Sons, fueled by capital raised on the stock market, and buoyed by the market access of the British Empire, the Scotch industry was enjoying a golden age in the late 19th century. At the center of this rapidly expanding Scotch boom were the Pattinson brothers.

Starting out as a pair of dairy farmers, Robert and Walter Pattinson began a blending company in 1887, which they took public in 1889, raising $19.8 million in 2023 dollars. When one considers that all that money was for two blended whisky brands that were not even three years old, the story already starts to look very much like one of today's Wall Street tech stock boondoggles.

The brothers spent this windfall acquiring stakes in Aultmore, Glenfarclas, and Oban distilleries, but mostly this and other borrowed monies were used in promoting their brands. Their most famous publicity stunt was giving out 500 grey parrots that had been trained to croak "Buy Pattinson's Whisky" to grocers and publicans. Another point with modern parallels was the brothers' lavish lifestyles: they bought country estates, maintained regal offices, and traveled ostentatiously in private trains.

Yet, the Pattinsons were speeding toward the expected trainwreck. Their empire was largely based on the overvaluation of their whisky stockpile, which they helped inflate by buying previously sold stocks back at higher prices. Not to mention the company was also a Ponzi scheme, paying dividends to investors not with profits, but by drawing on borrowed or existing company capital.

By 1898, the industry was headed for a downturn regardless, because the 1890s' Scotch boom had led to substantial overproduction. The Pattinsons' machinations helped turn what might have been a market correction into a full-blown crash. On December 5, their stock price imploded by 55 percent, which set the dominoes tumbling. The Pattinsons fell, and they took several other suppliers and creditors down with them.

But the damage didn't stop there because the scandal dragged whisky prices further. The fallout of the Pattinson crash shuttered many distilleries and put a halt to new distilleries. This slump led into World War I, the Great Depression, and World War II. All told, there wouldn't be a new distillery built in Scotland until 1949!

The brothers were accused, tried, and convicted of fraud and embezzlement. Robert spent eighteen months in prison, and Walter served a nine-month term.

HOW TWO BROTHERS WROTE THE BOOK AND BUILT THE BRAND ON DEWAR'S

The telling of how Dewar's got its start has so many elements in common with other big brands of blended Scotch whisky that they all tend to jumble together in my memory, and I need to look up the details every time to keep them straight. After getting past the origins, though, Dewar's is an easy one to remember, because it's an account involving presidents and the creation of a classic cocktail.

John Dewar was an ambitious wine and spirits merchant, who founded his own company and store in 1846. Part of his business was buying and blending Scottish whiskies in an era when the popular spirits with the middle and upper classes were cognac and Irish whiskey. But after 1880, the task of taking Dewar's whiskies from Scotland to the world fell to his sons, John Alexander and Tommy Dewar.

Whether it came naturally by disposition or by agreement, the pair had a division of labor that propelled the Perth, Scotland, firm forward. John A. Dewar looked after the nuts and bolts of the business, while Tommy Dewar took on sales and marketing.

Dewar's had established a major presence in London pubs and restaurants by 1890, when they received a request from the industrialist and philanthropist Andrew Carnegie to send a cask of whisky to President Benjamin Harrison. Carnegie had previously sent Dewar's to the inauguration of President James A. Garfield, but for some reason it's the gift of whisky to Harrison that everyone remembers, perhaps because Garfield was assassinated after six months in office. Regardless, the more famous Harrison consignment of Scotch gave the brand a boost in the American market, becoming the first real step in establishing Dewar's enduring popularity in America. Through the 20th century and into the 21st, the brand has often been either the first or second best-selling Scotch whisky in the US (it is currently number two, after Johnnie Walker).

This international success inspired Tommy Dewar to go on his first world sales tour, from 1892 to 1894. Over the course of those two years, the junior Dewar visited 26 countries, appointing local salesmen in his wake. By the time he was done, Dewar's was a globally exported whisky. He wrote an applauded book about his journey, *A Ramble Round the Globe*, wherein Dewar claims to have invented the Highball while visiting New York.

John Dewar Jr. hadn't been idle while Tommy was building a global sales team. In 1893, he won a Royal Warrant from Queen Victoria, becoming the first of many Scotch whiskies to do so. More substantially, in 1898 he opened Aberfeldy Distillery, whose malt whisky has been at the heart of Dewar's ever since. However, neither Dewar brother was behind the creation of Dewar's White Label, still the company's entry-level, top-selling blended whisky, in 1899. That was the work of their first master blender, A. J. Cameron. Today that role is occupied by Stephanie Macleod, who has been master blender at John Dewar & Sons since 2006.

WAS THE GLENFIDDICH REALLY THE FIRST SINGLE MALT?

One night, my now ex-wife and I were curled up and watching a Brit crime show, an episode of Geraldine McEwan's *Marple*. In the latter stages of the story, Vicar Septimus Bligh and co-sleuth Tuppence share why each of them is an alcoholic, but before so doing so Septimus suggests a tipple. "A little of The Glenfiddich?" he offers.

I groaned and rolled my eyes. That episode was set in the immediate aftermath of post-war Britain, something one could tell by various cues: the B-17s that flew away and the American bomber crews still wearing green, not the blue they would adopt in 1949. The stickler in me winced at the error, this in a show that otherwise very much looked the part, because that bottle Bligh proffered to Tuppence is actually a famous one. It's famous because The Glenfiddich is the original single malt, the very first marketed as such.

The closest thing the sad vicar could have offered at the time

was Grant's Stand Fast, made by William Grant & Sons. The namesake William Grant is also the founder of The Glenfiddich Distillery, and in the 1950s Grant's Stand Fast was their bestseller. But William Grant's great-grandchildren, Charlie and Sandy Grant, recognized they were in an industry seeing hard times and fierce competition. If the company was going to survive, they needed to differentiate themselves from their rivals.

Their first move was to introduce the triangular bottle in 1961, which continues to be the mark of both Grant's and The Glenfiddich. In an early example of telling the story of whisky with its physical container, the triangle represents the trinity of whisky: water, air, and barley. The bottle shape has come to be as iconic as the squared bottle of Jack Daniel's or the red wax of Maker's Mark.

Yet their revolutionary move came in 1963, when they introduced The Glenfiddich Straight Malt. As has been exhaustively documented, this was not the first example of a single malt whisky being sold. I think the most famous evidence disproving the claim that The Glenfiddich was the literal first single malt is that the dissolute King George IV was famously fond of The Glenlivet, even before it became legal and prior to the invention of blends that needed grain whisky. The most ironic disproof is how, according to whisky author Ian Buxton, The Macallan was selling 15-year-old whisky in England in the same year The Glenfiddich Straight Malt was introduced.

But a number of factors made The Glenfiddich venture different. The most important was that it was marketed and sold outside of not just Scotland, but outside of Britain. The Scotch business has been heavily reliant on exports from its very beginnings, so selling something just in Scotland or even Britain is akin to a bourbon release being Kentucky-only. If Elmer T. Lee had kept Blanton's at home in the 1980s, nobody would care about the single barrel bourbon today.

Moreover, the Grants understood the importance of telling a good story to sell a good drink. Their foundation was the idea that provenance matters in whisky, and from there they built up the mythology of their distillery in the Valley of the Deer, talked about the quality of water coming from their spring, and advanced the idea of the single malt whisky. A quote attributed to Charlie Grant, something he is supposed to have said when he was traveling around the world with The Glenfiddich, is "dram by dram, bartender by bartender, bar by bar, we will grow single malt whisky." That could be the mission statement of every brand ambassador in the business today.

LIVING LEGEND: SIR DAVID STEWART

When I am asked about the Scottish equivalent of Elmer Lee or Jimmy Russell, I have a ready answer: David Stewart. Like Russell, he is a living legend of the trade, and his career milestones are of an era strikingly similar to those of his peers.

Stewart began apprenticing at William Grant & Sons in 1962 at the age of 17. That was a propitious time, because the next year their distillery The Glenfiddich would start marketing a new expression that would revolutionize the Scotch whisky industry: the single malt.

Twelve years later, Stewart was appointed as a malt master in the company. By this time, the single malt had become an industry-wide standard, as dozens of distilleries had followed suit. However, it was also the mid-1970s, which was when the whiskey industry around the world began to experience a steep decline in demand, leading to the Great Whiskey Bust. Like his American peers, Stewart would play a key role in crafting some of the innovations that would lead to the revival of his industry.

In the 1980s, Stewart developed the idea of two-cask maturation, also called secondary maturation, but better known to drinkers as "finishing." In this process, the whisky gets its primary maturation as usual, which in the Scotch industry usually (but not always) means in an ex-bourbon barrel or a hogshead built from recycled ex-bourbon barrels. After this first, standard round, the whisky is then transferred to another barrel that is fresh from being used to mature some other type of liquor. The wood fibers are still soaked with that liquor, imparting the influence of it upon the whisky. Stewart employed this process to make whiskies great and small, like The Balvenie Classic, Grant's Ale Cask, and Grant's Sherry Cask. Finishing has since spread from the Scotch industry into world whiskey as a whole; distillers as disparate as Angel's Envy in Kentucky and Kavalan in Taiwan are built on finishing as their foundational concept.

Another far-reaching innovation of Stewart's was the importation of solera aging from the Spanish sherry industry. Although the exact details will vary from solera to solera, the idea is that one has a cask or vat full of maturing liquor. When the maturation cycle has reached its fruition, only part of the vessel's contents is emptied. It is then topped up with new liquid.

Stewart's own version built on his two-cask maturation. He started with Glenfiddich malt whisky aged for at least 15 years in ex-sherry and ex-bourbon casks, finishing the latter in new American oak barrels. Then both sets, the ex-sherry and ex-bourbon, are dumped and "married" in a specially built oak vat. That is the solera. It is never fully emptied, so in theory traces of every fill of the vat since it was started in 1998 are still there. As with finishing, solera aging caught on with other whiskey makers around the world.

Stewart began stepping down from his overarching role at William Grant & Sons in 2009, when he handed over the jobs of malt master at Glenfiddich and master blender at Grant's to Brian Kinsman. In 2016, the British Crown recognized Stewart's achievements by granting him an MBE. Finally, after 49 years as a malt master at the company, Stewart handed his duties at The Balvenie over to Kelsey McKechnie in August 2023, but he continues as The Balvenie's Honorary Ambassador. Again, very much like his peers in America, the living legend might step back, but he is just too esteemed to step away.

DO YOU PREFER A SQUAT BOTTOM OR A LONG, GRACEFUL NECK?

Only in the most industrial of settings does the copper still fail to stand out as a thing of beauty. Modern distilleries are consciously designed to emphasize this. Pay a visit to The Glenlivet stillhouse, and one is confronted by rows of gleaming copper pots enclosed by floor-to-ceiling windows on two sides, offering a panorama of the rolling countryside and imposing hills of Scotland (and those are hills around The Glenlivet, not mountains). But even in less grand settings, the polished copper pot still retains its allure, so much so that I refer to pictures of stills as "copper porn."

But copper pots have something to them that column stills do not, which adds to their romance. A column still might be a beautiful machine, but it looks very much like a machine, and the kind of whisky it makes can be summarized with the responses to the following questions: How many plates does it have? What is its diameter? How tall is it? One describes a pot still in different and more artful terms.

This is because the pot still is both a simple and complicated device. The bottom half is basically a pot, as the name indicates. This is where the mash or wort is heated, causing (mostly) the alcohol to vaporize and rise. That vapor rising into the neck starts the complicated part.

Alcohol is a colorless, odorless, and tasteless substance, and it's the oils and other compounds in the mash and wort that give a new make whiskey its flavor. Also, some water vaporizes. The taller and slimmer the neck, the more this vaporous mixture will separate as it rises. Lagavulin is a famous example, because its stills have a squat, conical neck that produces a quite hefty new make whisky. If the still is fabricated with a long, thin neck, the new make comes out lighter. This design is what The Glenmorangie is known for, and its stills are as tall as a giraffe. Cognoscenti might describe a pear-shaped still with a low, conical neck as dumpy, and one with a towering, slender neck as rakish.

Another way to achieve the same effect as a tall neck is to put a narrow waist at its base. This half-constriction helps separate the vapor from the simmering mash or wort, calming it down and allowing it to separate more easily. The stills at The

GLENFIDDICH

4550 LITRES

SPIRIT STILL Nº

GL

S

Glenlivet have rather modest examples of that waisted neck, while at The Glenkinchie the waists are more pronounced.

Another easy-to-identify design feature is the reflux sphere, a spherical bulge sometimes built into the base of the neck. The additional surface area in the sphere allows more heat to bleed out of that sphere, producing the reflux of condensation: droplets of heavier stuff, like water, form in the sphere and the lower part of the neck, and flow back down into the pot. This preserves the upper part of the neck for the separation of the lighter elements in the vapor. The design combines a waisted base for the neck, a reflux sphere, and a rakish upper neck, maximizing separation.

These differences in design are why no two distilleries in Scotland are the same, not even on the inside, and why every one of the over 140 single malt whiskies is distinctive, even as a new make. With most distilleries using the same varietal of barley and a standardized yeast, it is the still design that makes each new make distinctive.

WILL THE REAL GLENLIVET PLEASE STAND UP?

The passage of the Excise Act of 1823 cleared the path for Scottish whisky makers to transition from de facto moonshiners to the beginnings of an industry. George Smith

of the River Livet Valley, Glen Livet, was well prepared to seize the moment because the next year he secured the very first distilling license issued under the act. Smith was an illicit distiller prior to 1824, so he had the knowledge and the starter equipment on hand, but I've long suspected that his being first was more than just a coincidence. His landlord was the Duke of Gordon, the very same man who proposed the Excise Act. Thus, I believe it is a good guess that Smith was informed of Gordon's intentions and made his preparations in advance, such as mustering the cash to pay for his license.

It's known that King George IV, a famously dissolute man, was fond of Glenlivet whisky, having tried some during an 1822 visit. The Glenlivet founded by George Smith has laid claim to that preference as part of its origin story, but it is impossible to know for sure if the whisky the monarch was given was made by Smith. When George IV came calling in Edinburgh, "Glenlivet" was a generic term being used to describe whiskies made nowhere near the glen of the River Livet.

The term Glenlivet was still in widespread usage by many distillers to describe their products when, in 1852, Charles Dickens sent a parcel of whisky to a friend, with a letter encouraging him to try the "rare old Glenlivet." I want to believe that Dickens would have understood the difference between the distillery actually in Glen Livet and all the others borrowing the name, but the case still isn't rock solid.

The Smith family didn't trademark the term until 1870, and they spent 1882 to 1884 in court trying to expensively sue other users into quitting their use of the name Glenlivet. The result was a settlement where only the Smith's distillery could call itself "The Glenlivet," while the others had to use a hyphenated name, and into the 20th century even a distillery as distinguished as The Macallan was still labeling its products as Macallan-Glenlivet. The distillery set up by the Smiths has always been the first and only legal one operating by the Livet, but it had to fight long and hard to claim its name away from literally dozens of competitors.

THE PEOPLE BEHIND
THE WALKER

Johnnie Walker is not just the best-selling Scotch whisky, but the top-selling brand of whiskey of any stripe or description. While brand founder John Walker was a real person, the company's famous striding logo isn't Walker, however much it takes its cue from his name. That aspirational figure was created in 1908 by cartoonist Tom Browne in a moment of inspiration. Over lunch with one of the Walker's directors, Lord Stevenson, Browne sketched the Striding Man on the back of a menu.

The logo itself is therefore just a bit of aspirational commercial art that has evolved over the years, keeping pace with the times, and growing into something iconic. But some of the people who were behind that evolution were remarkable characters in their own right. Browne himself did not get to oversee his creation for long, as he had cancer and died from surgical complications in 1910 at just 39 years old. The journey of the Striding Man was carried forward by many others.

His immediate successor was Sir Bernard Partridge, who had just become the chief cartoonist for *Punch* magazine. He consolidated Browne's work in the pre–World War I years but was soon occupied with other concerns. Working for *Punch*, Partridge had already produced some of the most famous British political cartoons of the first half of the 20th century and would soon go on to create iconic recruitment posters for the war effort.

After the patriotic imagery of the First World War era and the return to aspirational themes afterward, the look of the Striding Man got a splash of color and joined the Art Deco era when Doris Zinkeisen took over the illustrator's duties from 1927 to 1928. There are books in print today dedicated to her work as an artist, and she was commissioned with her sister to do the murals on the RMS *Queen Mary*; you can take a peek if you are ever in Long Beach, California. It was Zinkeisen who made the Striding Man's coat red.

The Striding Man took on its recognizable "Keep Walking" shape during a facelift in 1999. It was given some further tweaking by Gary Redford in 2015, and it has been said Redford finally took the figure the rest of the way from Edwardian dandy to full-on Mr. Darcy. Redford's work is akin to that actor whose name you don't know, but you certainly recognize it on sight. If you go through his portfolio, you'll find plenty of familiar images beyond the current Johnnie Walker logo.

THE MONKEY'S SHOULDER

Monkey Shoulder is a Scotch whisky with two stories, one Dickensian and the other technical, but a little bit of both tales are present right there on the bottle. The triple set of monkeys, with their curled tails, and the name point straight to an old-fashioned practice in the whisky and brewing industries: floor malting.

Malt is germinated barley, and germination is the necessary first step in fermenting that barley. The grain is spread out on a stone or concrete floor and wetted down, allowing nature to do its work, but not exactly take its course. Every eight hours or so, someone needs to go onto a malting floor and turn the grain over with a scoop shovel, to prevent the germinated barley from sprouting roots.

This turning occurs every several hours for four or five days. Given the quantities involved, there would often be more than one malting floor, and the process rarely stopped, even in winter. Peated whiskies are an accidental side effect of the floor malting process because many distilleries would burn peat to keep the malting rooms warm. The peat smoke would permeate the grain, and from there find its way into the whisky. Bending over and working the scoop shovel to turn the malt day in, day out caused a repetitive strain injury that left an arm dangling, kind of like a monkey's, hence, monkey shoulder. It's an old-fashioned process, and nowadays malting barley is usually outsourced, though some distillers who want to emphasize a more traditional process continue to do floor maltings.

The technical story is told by the terms on the label, "Batch 27" and "Blended Malt." Monkey Shoulder is a triple malt that represents William Grant & Sons bringing together three of their four malt distilleries: Glenfiddich, Balvenie, and Kininvie. Whereas a blended whisky, such as Johnnie Walker, brings together malt whisky and grain whisky, a blended malt has no grain whisky. These whiskies used to be called vatted malts, a term meant to differentiate them from blended whiskies, but that term's use has fallen out of favor. Batch 27 refers to the recipe the blenders chose for Monkey Shoulder, so it's clear that they had at least 27 variants of the three malts (perhaps more) going in the lab.

Introduced in 2003, Monkey Shoulder is still sometimes referred to as "innovative" or "revolutionary," which it is most definitely not. Although a fine bottle of malt whisky, double malts and triple malts (blends of two or three malts) are nothing new. I first read about them in an in-flight magazine on my first trip abroad, to London in 1989. Being 18, I promptly ordered one when I arrived, so a vatted malt was the first Scotch whisky I ever tried.

THE WOMAN BLENDING SOME OF THE WORLD'S OLDEST WHISKY

If Kirsteen Campbell's career path to date has been archetypal of the Scotch industry, the position she holds now is anything but. For the last few years, she has been master whisky maker at The Macallan, arguably the most prestigious of all single malts. When I read of her promotion to working on The Macallan in 2019, my thought was that women had well and truly arrived in making Scotch whisky.

Campbell hails from Thurso, a small town with a population of roughly 7,300 that lies on the north coast of the Highlands, looking out towards Orkney. Dunnet Head, the northernmost point in mainland Scotland, is a 25-minute drive away. She graduated with a bachelor's degree in food science from Glasgow Caledonian University and earned a diploma from the Institute of Brewing and Distilling at Heriot-Watt University, a proper educational foundation for anyone working in the whisky-making trade. She went straight into the booze business in 2001, landing a job in a laboratory analyzing new make vodka, gin, rum, and whisky for a spirits company. Her fascination for Scotch whisky began at this time, as she appreciated its complexity, even in a new make form, relative to the rum or vodka she had been focusing on. She did a stint at the Scotch Whisky Research Institute in Edinburgh, before taking a job with Edrington.

That move to Edrington, the parent company of The Macallan, came in October 2007. After a few years of similar lab work as a quality technologist, Campbell was promoted to master blender for Cutty Sark, becoming the steward of a brand for the first time. During that period, she created a handful of Cutty Sark whiskies, including Cutty Sark Prohibition, an affordable blended whisky I'm rather fond of.

After more than five years working on Cutty Sark, she was made master blender for The Famous Grouse, a somewhat more prestigious blended whisky brand. When I asked her about what the difference between the two blends was, she said, "In broad terms, Cutty has more flavor influence from American oak sherries (vanilla, citrus, toffee notes), whilst The Famous Grouse leans more towards European oak sherries (dried fruits, spicy notes)." The Famous Grouse draws on malts from Glenturret, Highland Park, and, of course, The Macallan.

Campbell has been leading the whisky-making team at The Macallan for four years now, much celebrated as the first woman to take the helm at that high-profile brand. It's part of a larger trend in an industry noted for its commitment to tradition, which began when Rachel Barrie became the first female master blender in the industry in 2011 (Barrie currently makes Benriach, GlenDronach, and Glenglassaugh). At one point, half of Campbell's own team of six at The Macallan was made up of women.

Just a couple of weeks before I started typing this profile, it was announced that a bottle of "the world's most valuable whisky" would be put up for auction at Sotheby's, part of a lot of 40 bottles of The Macallan drawn from sherry casks that were filled in 1926 and bottled at age 60 in 1986. This ultrarare whisky was tested against another sample of 1926 Macallan held by Edrington to prove authenticity and quality, and it was Kirsteen Campbell signing off on what Sotheby's Head of Spirits called "the most desirable bottle of whisky ever to come onto market."

WAS THE CLASSIC <u>1984</u> FUELED BY SCOTCH?

The way I've often heard it told, the greatest work of dystopian fiction ever published was written on an intersection of Scotch and isolation. When George Orwell needed to get away from it all, he chose Jura. That Hebridean island is noteworthy for its deer outnumbering the people by about 25 to 1, and for the Jura Distillery. It is often said that he holed up in a farmhouse named Barnhill on Jura with a case of Scotch and did not emerge until the classic *1984* was written.

That legend hasn't quite become fact yet. It conjures a Hemingway-like image of Orwell, and in so doing leaves quite a bit of the real man and his circumstances out of the picture. Orwell was a recent widower when he first arrived on Jura in 1946, and he went with his adopted son, Eric, in tow. Sometimes his sister and her children were there, as well. The author was suffering from tuberculosis at the time; the disease would claim his life shortly after the publication of *1984*. He also lived on Jura off and on for two and a half years, and not in one continuous go.

But the other elements of the story are true enough. Orwell liked a good drink, and one must bring their own supplies and be well-stocked to live at Barnhill, so no doubt there was a case of Scotch brought along on one of those stays. Also, the whisky distillery that was working there in the mid-to-late 1940s is still open today. If Orwell ever bought some whisky from Jura, no one knows. To mark the year of their island's most famous product, Jura laid up 1,984 casks of malt whisky in 1984. Thirty years later, they bottled the single malt as Jura 1984.

Barnhill is still very much what it was when Orwell lived there. The concessions to modernity seem forced upon the Fletcher family, who were Orwell's hosts and still own the house: a generator to supply power for lights and chargers, and a gas-powered refrigerator. The sources of warmth (and you'll need warmth there, because daytime highs peak at 60 degrees Fahrenheit in July) remain as they were in Orwell's time: a hefty cast-iron stove and a dram of whisky.

MIDLETON

Tourists who come to the seat of Jameson Irish Whiskey see, for the most part, Old Midleton. The buildings and grounds of the original distillery are now the visitor center and constitute the entire experience. For a historic industrial site in Ireland, Old Midleton is expansive (compare it to Kilbeggan, if you ever get the chance to visit). James Murphy & Co. bought the property from its namesake, Viscount Midleton, in 1825 with the ambition of building the largest distillery in Ireland. That fact is underlined by the gigantic copper pot still that greets visitors upon arrival. The gargantuan 31,618-gallon still is the largest ever made. At a time when most whiskey distilleries in any country were still small affairs run by farmers, the Murphy operation employed 200 people.

Adjacent to this is New Midleton, which is very much a product of the nadir of Irish whiskey, while at the same time the symbol of its modern success. In 1966, three of Ireland's surviving whiskey makers—John Jameson & Son, John Powers & Son, and Cork Distilleries Company—merged to form Irish Distillers. Of their three plants (the Bow Street Distillery and John's Lane Distillery in Dublin, Old Midleton in Cork), none were fit to meet the demands of the new company. But unlike the others, Old Midleton had room for expansion, as it was not located in the midst of Ireland's largest city. The decision was made to close all the existing plants and consolidate around a new, purpose-built distillery in Cork.

The strategy was to focus on Jameson, which, as the lightest of the brands held by Irish Distillers, was deemed to have the best export potential. This choice was in parallel with American distillers developing and marketing light whiskey as part of their effort to chase drinkers who were imbibing vodka. Unlike light whiskey, Jameson has withstood the test of time.

However, Jameson was not the only thing made at New Midleton. Irish Distillers was, at one point, the monopolist of Irish whiskey. They became the owners of most every legacy brand in the country, including Bushmills, and everything that wasn't Bushmills was made at New Midleton for a time. Paddy, Powers, Midleton Very Rare, Redbreast, the Spots, and Tullamore Dew were all in-house brands at one time, and Knappogue Castle was acquired in 2021. Paddy and Tullamore Dew were sold in the middle 2010s, but New Midleton continued to supply them with stocks of whiskey for years thereafter.

New Midleton is also a major player in providing stock whiskey to other companies, so it plays at least a part in many other Irish whiskeys. As is the case in the Kentucky bourbon industry, this role is well-known, but the details are kept hazy. So, think on this: until the last few years, all pot still whiskey in Ireland was made by just New Midleton. Thus, any sourced brand using pot still whiskey could only have gotten it from there, whether the companies concerned choose to acknowledge it or not.

The work behind supporting these many brands means that Midleton's scope of operations is more like a big Kentucky or Japanese distillery than a distillery in Scotland, in that they

OLD MIDLETON

make several different distillates as a matter of regular practice. "On our main distillery, we generally produce three types of single pot still whiskey, with different aromas and flavors," according to Kevin O'Gorman, the master distiller at New Midleton. "We use the terms Light, Medium, and Heavy to describe the different flavor and aroma intensity, but the reality is that the three styles are quite different."

In addition to making three separate new makes of pot still whiskey, New Midleton also operates an in-house microdistillery, which is used for experiments and the production of malt whiskey. They also have an array of column stills employed in making grain whiskey. Just the one standard type of grain whiskey is made at New Midleton, but they are known to produce small runs of nonstandard grain whiskey, drawing on varying and distinct mash bills. To accomplish all of this, New Midleton employs ten pot stills divided between the Barry Crockett Stillhouse and the Garden Stillhouse, three more pot stills at the microdistillery, and six column stills.

Most of the vast output capacity is directed towards Jameson, which is the colossus of the Irish whiskey industry. When I first started writing about whiskey more than a decade ago, there were just four distilleries on the Emerald Isle: New Midleton, Bushmills, Cooley, and Kilbeggan. Today the number is over forty, but that hasn't changed Jameson's outsized footprint in its category. In 2020, 73 percent of all the Irish whiskey sold was Jameson.

That figure is just Jameson brand whiskeys, not Redbreast, Powers, Midleton Very Rare, or anything else made at New

Midleton. Nowhere else in the world does one distillery make such an enormous mark on its regional or national category. It's a fair statement to say that the identity of modern Irish whiskey is what Irish Distillers decided it would be, and that vision was made reality at New Midleton.

HOW THWARTING THE TAXMAN INVENTED IRELAND'S SIGNATURE WHISKEY

Single pot still whiskey is a uniquely Irish style of whiskey making, and the story behind it is typically Irish. As the name indicates, this whiskey is made in a pot still, but so is the malt whiskey from which the style is derived. Like so much else in the history of any former British possession, single pot still whiskey came into being from that most patriotic desire to thwart the grasping will of the Crown.

Even in the 18th century, Ireland was known to have a thriving distillation industry. The problem for the British exchequer was how to collect taxes on all that spirited business. Irish distillers were already taxed by the volume of their stills and on the amount of spirit produced, but the latter was hard to measure with so many working distilleries, even on a small island like Ireland. So, in 1785 the British slapped a new tax, the Malt Tax, going directly after the source grain almost all the booze in Ireland was made out of.

Irish history between 1798 and 1804 was marked by repeated uprisings, but none of these were sparked by steep taxes on making liquor. Instead, the Irish responded by trying to outwit the revenuers. If malted barley was taxed, then they would simply use less of it, and thus single pot still whiskey came into being. The style continued to be made in pot stills, as with the precursor malt whiskey, but now with a mix of malted and unmalted barley. At times, other untaxed grains (most often rye) were used. The result was whiskey with a creamy mouthfeel, robust body, and spicy flavor.

Pot still whiskey became the engine that drove Irish dominance of the world whiskey market. By 1835, around the time Scotch and bourbon production was becoming recognizable by modern standards, Ireland was home to 93 licensed distilleries, and most of the whiskey and other spirits made were exported. Irish pot still whiskey was the most popular style of whiskey in the world. Far from stifling Irish whiskey, British taxes (and the work-arounds devised to avoid them) drove Irish distilling to ascendancy.

Ironically, it was an Irish invention that undermined their own supremacy in the world's whiskey trade. Irishman Aeneas Coffey perfected the design for the continuous column still, patented his work, and his name is interchangeable with the column still even to this day. Coffey's still was more efficient to operate than a pot still, but this didn't mean the Irish industry was keen to adopt it.

This is sometimes portrayed as the Irish whiskey business being hidebound and set in their ways (certainly that was the way it was told at the Irish Whiskey Museum when I went there, shortly after they opened their doors). But that doesn't sound like the whole truth. Column stills tend to produce lighter bodied whiskey, which defeats much of the point of the pot still style, and the pot still style is what Irish whiskey's identity was built on.

But across the Irish Sea lay a distilling industry still just recently legalized, and the Scots adopted Coffey's new technology to great effect. They used the column still to make grain whisky, which they combined with their existing malt whisky to create blended whisky. Those more approachable, cheaper to make blended whiskies gave rise to a peer competitor for the Irish whiskey industry.

IS BUSHMILLS REALLY THE WORLD'S OLDEST WHISKEY DISTILLERY?

When the drink in your tumbler could be decades old, that lends itself pretty well to attaching tales of antique origins and practices. This is why the folks in Scotland and Ireland will sometimes speak of their medieval *usquebaugh* or *uisce beatha*, the very distant ancestor to today's whiskeys, even though my experience with moonshine tells me very few people actually want to drink Celtic aqua vitae.

Even better than pointing to an ancient tradition is having a genuinely ancient distillery, and Bushmills lays claim to having the oldest whiskey distillery in the world. How true that claim is depends on how one defines "oldest," and there are partisans who debate this.

Bushmills (named for the mills on the adjacent River Bush) traces its lineage back to when Sir Thomas Phillips, the British governor of County Antrim, was granted a royal license to distill whiskey in 1608. But the Bushmills Old Distillery Company wasn't founded until 1784. Distillery operations through the course of the nineteenth century are not clear, and Bushmills may have been closed at different times, but it definitely burned to the ground in 1885. Although the distillery was swiftly rebuilt following that fire, it clearly wasn't making whiskey in the interim.

This history matters, to some anyway, because Scotch whisky has some especially passionate advocates. Their argument, which I first became acquainted with at Spirit of Speyside one year, is as follows: 1) the 1608 license doesn't matter, because it has nothing to do with Bushmills; 2) the 1784 date that actually applies to Bushmills doesn't matter, because the distillery has been closed at times, maybe repeatedly and for long periods of time; 3) therefore the distillery that is properly entitled to the claim as the world's oldest is Strathisla, which has been in continuous operation since 1786. The "continuous operation" part is critical to the point because otherwise Bushmills still has a valid claim of one type or another to the title. Note that this hair-splitting argument isn't advanced by Strathisla itself.

The claim is even disputed in Ireland, where some folks prefer to point to Kilbeggan as the oldest distillery in the country (and, by extension, the world). It is well-established that the Kilbeggan Distillery was started in 1757, although the facility was shuttered for long stretches a couple of times in its history. When John Cooley brought it back to life in 2007, the building was essentially a ruin.

This type of argument is fun, in much the same way that talking about whether Jack Daniel's is bourbon or not is a classic American bar debate. As a practical matter, the 1608 royal license exists, and Bushmills can (tenuously) trace its legacy back to it. In much the same way, Michter's can trace a legacy all the way back to a Mennonite farmer named John Shenk, who founded a Pennsylvania distillery in 1753 and is said to have provided whiskey to shivering patriots at Valley Forge.

There is truth, history, and "marketing truth," and marketing truth is meant to be the better story. So, the answer to whether Bushmills is actually the oldest whiskey distillery in the world is "it depends." That said, the argument that it isn't requires more quibbling than I care to make.

IRISH SCOTCH AND SCOTCH-IRISH WHISKEY

The signature of Irish whiskey is supposed to be triple distillation. The triple set of gleaming copper stills is a familiar sight in Ireland. That Woodford Reserve in Kentucky adopted an Irish-style triple set of pot stills is very much part of that bourbon maker's charm. But Irish law says nothing about triple distillation, and it's certainly not required to make malt and pot still whiskeys.

Wrestling with long decades of decline, Irish Distillers started looking for ways to differentiate their product from Scotch during the 1960s. One that they hit upon was their practice of triple distillation, which produced a lighter, smoother whiskey. By the 1970s and 1980s, Irish Distillers was the only company making whiskey in all of Ireland, because at that time they owned both surviving distilleries on the Emerald Isle: New Midleton and Bushmills. Both plants were triple distillers.

Yet (the Republic of) Ireland's second distillery rejected that premise. When John Teeling opened Cooley Distillery in 1989, he was basically challenging a monopoly, and Teeling chose to make his malt whiskey using double distillation. I've heard jokes on many occasions that Teeling, who lectured at University College Dublin's business school for over 20 years and was known to have a shrewd head for business years before he got into the whiskey trade, went that way because it was cheaper. There may be some truth to the jibe, but it is also said that the only people in triple distillation in the 1980s were Irish Distillers, and they weren't sharing their know-how. When Teeling wanted to set up Cooley, most of the technical help he got came from Scotland, and Scotland does double distillation.

Despite that, this national identification with double or triple distilling is so much the case that when Cooley released Connemara, a peated, double-distilled Irish single malt, the wags pronounced it "Irish Scotch." In an even stronger indicator of how deeply triple distillation runs in the world of Irish whiskey, John Teeling's sons have a triple set of pot stills at their own distillery, Teeling Whiskey Company.

Conversely, that effort by Irish Distillers to distinguish themselves has led many to think of Scotch whisky as naturally being double distilled. But over in Scotland, Auchentoshan underlines that it was very much part of the Lowland whisky tradition to triple distill whisky. For decades, they were the only distillery in Scotland doing this, leading to the reverse joke: they were making Scotch whiskey (with an Irish "e"). But in July 2023, Rosebank Distillery was revived after 30 years of closure, complete with a triple still set. Also, Benriach and Benromach sometimes make triple-distilled whiskies. In America, Woodford Reserve has been making triple-distilled bourbon since the 1990s.

Historically, Irish whiskey was triple and double distilled, peated and unpeated, made with grains other than barley, and all manner of different things. Connemara is really a throwback, not an Irish imitation of Scotch. Triple distillation is very much the Irish style now, but that is exactly what it is: a style. And as we all know, styles can and do change.

IF YOU WORK IN WHISKEY, A SMOKE BREAK COULD KILL YOU SOONER, NOT LATER

Most people visit Jameson through their Bow Street visitor center in Dublin, and although it is billed as the "world's leading distillery tour," that facility is no longer actually making whiskey. For that, one must venture to Cork County and the New Midleton Distillery, which is home to Jameson, Redbreast, Powers, and much else besides. That includes one particularly interesting artifact: the Punishment Book of the old Bow Street distillery.

The notion of a log for workplace misdemeanors and exacted penalties sounds Dickensian, but in a sense the book was really about dealing with yesteryear's two most ordinary substance abuse problems: tobacco and alcohol. The Punishment Book dates back to an era when most everybody smoked, and smoking is problematic for a distillery for exactly the same reason it would be while standing at the gas pump. Distilleries are full of liquid alcohol, which is flammable enough in its own right, but even worse is that a still leak could mean a plume of invisible, highly flammable alcohol vapor is in the air.

Illicit smoking was the most common infraction, and a shockingly dangerous one, but workers were also sometimes caught helping themselves to whiskey on the job, either through the dipping dog or filling their own bottles and smuggling them home. The latter was the most serious offense, since it meant both stealing from the company *and* the taxman.

Employees of the distillery used to be given a daily whiskey ration, consisting of one dram at the beginning of the workday and another at the end. The most common punishment was the stoppage of this ration, either for a day, a few days, or a fortnight (two weeks). This was milder than docking a worker's pay, which punished both the employee and his family.

The idea of whiskey as part of the compensation package for distillery workers even extended to their pensions, and unlike the daily ration, that practice continues to this day. It's not uncommon to hear that retired, long-serving hands of the New Midleton Distillery get a monthly bottle of whiskey sent to their house. It's not an unheard of practice in the industry, even outside of Ireland. Jack Daniel's employees periodically get bottles of whiskey from the company, too.

WHEN WHISKEY BURNS,
IT BURNS BLUE

Industry is prone to calamity, and the whiskey industry is vulnerable to one type of calamity in particular: fire. It isn't hard to imagine why. Concentrated alcohol is a biofuel. Some of the ultrahigh proof, so-called "hazmat whiskeys" are strong enough to run a car on. A stillhouse might leak highly flammable, invisible alcohol vapors, and one should recall that the way spiritous liquors used to be "proofed" was by seeing if gunpowder wetted by them would fizzle, burn, or explode. In the whiskey industry, fires are often the most damaging of disasters, both in terms of property damage and in lives taken.

The Dublin Liberties Fire of 1875: Today, the Liberties district of Dublin is home to the Guinness Museum, Teeling Whiskey Company, the Pearse Lyons Distillery, and Roe & Co. Distillery. All these modern Irish booze makers basically came home, because in the late 19th century the district was also home to the whiskey industry, brewing, and the business that supported them.

On a Saturday evening in June 1875, a fire started in either Reid's malthouse or Malone's bonded warehouse, perhaps both. The former was stuffed with malted barley and the latter held 5,000 casks of whiskey, almost $7 million in goods between them. This pair of buildings were soon a de facto volcano, sending streams of burning, lavalike whiskey down Cork Street and into the surrounding neighborhood, where other houses and buildings caught fire. The blaze lasted only a single night, thanks to the quick reaction of the Dublin Fire Brigade.

Thirteen people died, but not one from the fire itself. Instead, they died from drinking out of the inches-deep flow of burning alcohol, either due to contamination or sheer alcohol poisoning.

The Luftwaffe Waged War on Scotch: Also known as the unluckiest distillery in Scotland, Banff Distillery in Aberdeenshire had already suffered a (more typical) fire in 1877, but was destined for an even darker fate. On August 16, 1941, a Junkers 88 bomber from the German air force bombed the distillery and hit Warehouse No. 12. Burning casks weighing hundreds of pounds were flung out, crashing through the walls and roof of the building, and burning whisky ran in streams down into the local watercourse. The next day, the local cows, ducks, and geese were all reported tipsy by their farmers.

Banff's ill fortune didn't stop with being victimized by the Nazis. A coppersmith, hard at work repairing a still, accidentally ignited vapors in the stillhouse, which caused an explosion. It was a gross safety violation, yet resulted in a relatively modest fine. The distillery soldiered on, shuttered only in 1983. In a final statement as to just how cursed Banff was, in 1991 the last standing building of the distillery burned to the ground before it could be demolished.

The Pekin, Illinois, Fire: When history dwells on fires in Illinois, the top of the list is the Chicago Fire of 1871, and for good reason. But as I often tell people when speaking to the history of whiskey in pre-Prohibition America, Peoria was once home to the largest whiskey distillery in the country, and distilling there revived after Prohibition and continued until the Great Whiskey Bust of the 1970s took it down. In 1954, three whiskey warehouses burned in a two-day fire that left six dead and more than thirty injured. As bad as that was, it could have been worse: the fire was prevented from spreading to neighboring warehouses, which held 220,000 more barrels of whiskey.

The Cheapside Whiskey Fire: The conflagration that struck Glasgow in 1960 wasn't just the worst whisky fire of the 20th century, but Britain's worst peacetime fire in the same era. Just as in Dublin, a fire got out of control in a bonded warehouse, one holding over one million gallons of high proof liquor (both whisky and rum). As the building shot blue flames high into the sky and spat explosions, it consumed most of what was around it, including an engine works, a tobacco warehouse, and an ice cream factory. Some 450 area firefighters were summoned to combat the inferno, and 19 of them died. The fire left a lasting impact on the city, and Glasgow fire service continues to hold memorials every March 28.

Heaven Hill Almost Burned to The Ground: As any true fan of Heaven Hill can tell you, the company might have ceased to exist in November 1996, in what is still Kentucky's most infamous distillery fire. Fanned by wind gusts of up to 75 mph, the flames soared to heights of 350 feet. Exploding barrels were seen flying through the air and, again, rivers of burning whiskey poured off the property. The inferno consumed the stillhouse, seven warehouses, and 90,000 barrels of whiskey. Scars of the fire are still visible on Heaven Hill's Bardstown property almost three decades later.

Yet this disaster also showed the Kentucky bourbon industry at its finest. Heaven Hill's peers rushed to their support, offering them whiskey stock and facilities to help them bridge the smoldering hole left in the company. The fire also set the stage for Heaven Hill's current split in facilities. Some of their warehouses, their bottling plant, and the visitor center are all on their old property in Bardstown. But the company chose to acquire a replacement distillery rather than rebuild the one that was razed, acquiring the Bernheim Distillery in Louisville.

Wild Turkey Ablaze: Three and a half years after the Heaven Hill fire, Wild Turkey suffered a smaller fire. Nonetheless, it was a damaging one, especially for the environment. One of their seven-story warehouses burned, sending flames 200 feet into the air and setting the surrounding woods alight. The warehouse held 17,000 barrels of bourbon, but most of it didn't fuel the blaze. Instead, the (now familiar) streams of burning whiskey rolled down the Kentucky River Palisades and into the river, where it poisoned the waters. Hundreds of thousands of fish were killed along a 66-mile stretch of the river, and regional drinking water systems were impaired.

The Silver Trail Explosion: Silver Trail was a small Western Kentucky legal moonshine distillery, owned by Spencer Ballantine, who had appeared in an early season of the Discovery Channel's *Moonshiners* as "that legal guy." Their equipment was built by an Oregon firm named Revenoor. This was one of many new still fabricators, springing up right behind the American craft distilling boom.

FIRE AT HEAVEN HILL IN NOVEMBER 1996

Revenoor's equipment failed, as detailed in the Kentucky fire marshall's investigation that followed the explosion and fire that struck Silver Trail in 2015. Two men were working in the stillhouse that day, a father and son team. The son was killed, and the father suffered severe burns. Ballantine, the owner of Silver Trail, sued Revenoor, which failed to respond to the lawsuit. Thus, Silver Trail won a default judgment.

Knowing those details, I couldn't help but wonder about other stills in operation around America and the world. Most were built by reputable firms, made by people who have been in the business of still making for decades—most, but not all. So, whenever I see my bottle of Silver Trail moonshine on the shelf, I'm always grateful that there hasn't been another such tragedy in the years since.

Jim Beam Warehouse Fire: The most recent major fire was at a Jim Beam property in Woodford County, where a rickhouse holding 45,000 barrels of whiskey ignited in a blaze that required fire companies from four Kentucky counties to extinguish. Worse than the sheer number of barrels was that the warehouse mostly held young whiskey, so all those barrels were either full or nearly so, as the angels had taken very little of their share. It was hot enough to melt the light casings on some of the fire trucks. Some runoff flowed into Glenn's Creek, a water source shared with Woodford Reserve and Castle & Key, as well as many frisky otters that I've become acquainted with over the years. Yet mercifully, no one was injured, and the fire was contained to the single rickhouse.

FLOODS, CRASHES, AND SPILLS, OH MY

Afire is easily the most dangerous type of misfortune that can befall a distillery, but other classes of mishaps are just as dramatic, if less life threatening. To American whiskey fans, probably the most famous example is a happy accident: the April 2006 tornado that tore much of the roof off of Buffalo Trace's Warehouse C. The incident also serves as a reminder as to how different things were for the Kentucky bourbon industry back then, because the same tornado demolished an empty warehouse nearby. The idea of any Buffalo Trace warehouse sitting empty today seems absurd.

The damaged building spent months without a roof, exposed to the rain, the upper tiers drenched in sunlight, and radically changing the ventilation of the building. The roof was repaired, years passed, and the barrels were sampled as they neared maturity for what was intended to be an installment of Colonel E. H. Taylor Small Batch. They discovered two things: the evaporation rate for the "tornado bourbon," as Buffalo Trace dubbed it, was more than doubled to an extreme "angel's share" of 63.9 percent. It was also ambrosia. The experience is said to have inspired the construction of Buffalo Trace's laboratory warehouse, designed so that light exposure, climate, and ventilation can all be controlled for experimental maturation.

Not all the tribulations at Buffalo Trace enjoy such happy endings. The distillery and its host city, Frankfort, sit on the banks of the Kentucky River, and flooding is a regular feature of working there. In 2017 and again in 2021, those parts of the distillery complex nearest the river were flooded. I witnessed a flood of the distillery and downtown Frankfort firsthand in 1989, but the worst was in 1978. That flood crested at 48½ feet, and routinely appears on lists of the worst floods in American history. If you know what to look for, you can still see signs of the floodmark on the riverbanks around Buffalo Trace.

But it seems the most common type of whiskey accident is the spill. Trucks hauling whiskey getting into accidents and losing at least some of their contents is an almost routine occurrence. In 2009, a tanker truck hauling 7,000 gallons of whiskey to the Jim Beam Distillery for bottling as Canadian Club overturned in Scott County, while in 2023 a truck carrying cases of Jack Daniel's on I-40 in Greensboro, Tennessee, got in a crash that wrecked the trailer, scattering the bottles across an exit ramp. There were many, many more in between.

Less common is when a warehouse collapses, as happened at Barton 1792 in 2018. Their Warehouse 30 was built in the 1940s and could store 18,000 barrels. In June of 2018, the building experienced structural failure, causing thousands of barrels to fall out of the building. It was estimated at the time that about a third of the total liquid volume of the building was spilled that day, which flowed into Withrow Creek. Like the Wild Turkey fire and spill, the contamination of the water with vast quantities of alcohol killed hundreds of fish.

Perhaps most dismaying for a whiskey lover is when simply opening the wrong valve accidentally dumps thousands of gallons of whiskey. In 2013, workers at the Chivas Brother's plant in Dumbarton, Scotland, thought they were emptying a tank of wastewater; instead, they poured an estimated 18,000 liters of aged Scotch into the sewers. Just a few years later, it was discovered that a storage vat at Loch Lomond's Catrine, Scotland, warehouse was leaking. By the time that leak was discovered, it is believed 60,000 liters of aged Scotch had trickled away.

LIVING LEGEND: BARRY CROCKETT

W hiskey is sometimes a family trade in more places than just Kentucky or Tennessee, but Barry Crockett's story is also much more than just a family legacy. His career charts the fall and resurrection of Irish whiskey itself.

Barry's father, Max Crockett, was the master distiller at the Old Midleton Distillery, the predecessor of today's central production plant for everything Irish Distillers makes. Barry was literally born there, in the distiller's cottage of Old Midleton, in 1948. Crockett would later say his father didn't insist on him going into the whiskey industry, but Ireland as a whole was "terribly depressed" at the time, so there weren't many other opportunities as promising as that one.

He succeeded his father in 1981 after a decade-long apprenticeship, taking the rudder at a time when his chosen industry

reached its lowest fortunes. The whiskey business had bottomed out, so much so that for the next several years Crockett was the steward of the sole whiskey distillery in the Republic of Ireland.

The timing was a pivot point for the identity of both Irish Distillers and Irish whiskey as a whole. New Midleton opened in 1975, so the middle and late 1970s were a period when Irish Distillers was consolidating their operations around their new central plant in Cork County. Their older stocks were drawn from the now-closed legacy distilleries, but the early work Barry and his father did together in getting the new distillery up and running was very much the future. One of the key decisions of that transition, when the son understudied with his father, was to continue making pot still whiskey. For decades, Midleton would be the only distillery to produce it.

Like his peers in America, Crockett began his personal legacy by creating new premium expressions that plotted a course out of the bottoms. The first was Midleton Very Rare, introduced in 1984. A couple of years later, the company acquired Redbreast, a single pot still brand that had been sourced through Irish Distillers. Crockett helped to relaunch Redbreast in 1991, beginning the revival of single pot still whiskey. The 21st century saw Crockett oversee the creation of new expressions at an accelerating pace as the whiskey boom picked up momentum, including the 2011 agreement with Mitchell & Sons to relaunch their single pot still brand, the Spots, and take it worldwide, starting with Green Spot. During this time, he was also training his eventual successor, Brian Nation.

After 47 years in the business, Barry Crockett retired in 2013, but Irish Distillers honored his achievements and long service two years prior with a namesake expression, Barry Crockett Legacy. This remains only the second expression from Irish Distillers to be named after a distiller, with the first being Jameson itself. Distinct from Crockett's other single pot still creations, his Legacy is matured in both ex-bourbon barrels and new white oak, with none of the wine cask influences that characterize the Spots and Redbreast.

FROM DJ TO DISTILLER

A certain pattern emerges when one reads the many pro-files of the people who become distillery managers and blenders in Ireland and Scotland. Typically, they go to university, study chemistry or engineering, and take a brief job in another field before breaking into the whiskey industry. From there, they steadily work their way up at the same company until achieving their first high profile role.

Then there is Lora Hemy. She didn't imagine a career in whiskey or even the sciences at university. Instead, Hemy went to art school and initially set out to be a painter. From there she found her way into sound engineering and DJ'ing in Dublin. But as Hemy tells it, she grew to find the two dimensions of painting dull to work with after a time, discovering sensory science instead. That led her into perfumery, which she was pursuing when she discovered whiskey on a visit to Glen Ord Distillery in Scotland. Realizing the role sensory science played in whiskey blending, she found a new North Star and began pursuing it: Hemy went back to school, enrolling in Heriot-Watt University's Institute of Brewing and Distilling.

After spending her twenties doing music, art, and perfumes, Hemy had the good timing to emerge from Heriot-Watt's program just as the Gin Boom was in full swing. She was hired by Halewood International and helped with establishing their initial distilleries before moving over to Atom Group, shifting from gin to whisky. And just as Hemy finished school at an opportune time, she likewise got her foot into the whiskey business at a perfect moment.

Irish whiskey has exploded like no other part of the business in the world in recent years, with the count of working whiskey distilleries on the island increasing by tenfold during the last decade. The international drinks goliath Diageo had previously gotten out of Irish whiskey altogether when they essentially traded Bushmills to Jose Cuervo. That company is well-known for its sometimes inexplicable moves, and only two years after swapping one of Ireland's two legacy whiskey distilleries for some tequila brands, Diageo decided to get back into the Irish whiskey game. They announced a new brand called Roe & Co., relying on sourced whiskey in the interim. Along with the new brand came plans to build a distillery in Dublin's The Liberties district, inside which was the powerhouse for the St. James's Gate Guinness Brewery. Diageo hired Hemy as head distiller at Roe & Co. in 2018.

Hemy had the virtue of having been engaged in the construction at Roe & Co. prior to taking the helm and running production there. She also gets to make whiskey from scratch, crafting an identity for a new brand in a new facility. It's still whiskey, though, so there is always that nod to the past. The old powerhouse is a 1940s era building, a sturdy industrial structure, so they had to work very much with the building in terms of renovations. With her artist's background, Hemy enjoys the architectural merits of her workplace. As she points out, "You can sit in our bar and literally look above and across into the old plant areas that we have retained on one side, and the distillery on the other." With its blend of old and new, innovation and tradition, the distillery certainly holds an iconic place along the Dublin skyline.

INDIA THREATENS TO DRINK THE WORLD'S WHISKY RESERVES DRY

According to some, the world's most consumed whisky comes not from Scotland or Kentucky, but India. Despite some of the country's most populous states having local Prohibition, the country consumes more whisky by volume than any other in the world. According to the Edinburgh Whisky Academy, one of every two bottles of whisky sold in the world is sold in India. That goes a long way towards explaining how four of the five top-selling whisky brands in the world are Indian.

But by a different measure, none of that is true. The wrinkle is that almost all of that Indian whisky isn't whisky at all, not according to international standards. All four of their top-selling brands mix imported whiskies and/or locally made whiskies with domestically produced neutral spirits made from sugarcane (rum, more or less).

If there is one point all the world's major whiskey-making traditions agree on for all its classes, distinctions, and categories, it is that whiskey is made from grain. So, when any of these nonwhiskies is exported, the labeling must be adjusted to call it "Indian Spirit" or something similar.

This isn't to say that India doesn't make real whisky, because the move to sell some of its domestically made malt whisky came in 2004, with the introduction of Amrut. Single malt brands like Amrut, Rampur, and Paul John are now exported, and bottles can be found alongside the malts of Scotland and Ireland across the US, Europe, and Asia. Alongside the exports and international recognition, demand at home for the Indian malts vastly exceeds supply. Nonetheless, India's single malts are still a drop in the bucket compared to the ersatz domestic "whiskies" that make up the bulk of the market.

This is why Johnnie Walker and Jack Daniel's are safely ensconced as the number one and two whiskey brands in the world. In the unlikely event that the powers that be decide it is OK to blend whisky with rum and still call it whisky, then Johnnie Walker would instantly drop to number five.

India's love of whisky is a legacy of the British Raj. "Scotch was favored by the British military officers and the nobility," says Raj Sabharwal, founding partner at Glass Revolution Imports. "Soon whisky became a symbol of taste and culture by the British Raj and the Indian elite. In 1820 Edward Dyer set up a brewery in northern India, and soon a distillery was added and the facility moved to Solan, near Simla, the summer home of the British. Solan Distillery still operates today." It mirrors cricket when you think about it: consumption of both whisky and cricket far outstrip anything going on back in Britain, both in absolute and relative terms. One can see the connection in the names of the many Indian whisky brands: Bagpiper, Royal Stag, Officer's Choice, Imperial Blue, and McDowell's.

I saw all of this for myself when I spent almost a year backpacking in India, and what I saw persuaded me that it was the vast thirst of India, not China, that was the future of exports of bourbon and Scotch. It probably would have been, too, were it not for India's determination to keep all that foreign whisky out. The current duty on foreign spirits is 150 percent!

Still, things are brightening for at least the Scotch whisky industry. Despite the trade barriers, demand for Scotch whisky is exploding in India. "In 2022, India became the largest export market for Scotch, surpassing France. Two hundred and nineteen million bottles of Scotch were sold in India in 2022 compared to 136 million in 2021, a remarkable growth," says Sabharwal. India and the UK are currently negotiating a free trade agreement, and one of the last sticking points is not just whether the whisky tariff was coming down, but by how much and how soon.

ABOUT THE AUTHOR

RICHARD THOMAS is the owner and managing editor of *The Whiskey Reviewer*, a leading web magazine for whiskey reviews, mixology, and trade news. Beyond his writing, Thomas's opinions and technical advice on whiskey have appeared in *Style* magazine, and in media outlets such as ABC News and the Discovery Channel. of the Lexington Cocktail Club. When not writing about whiskey, food, and travel, or working on his fiction, you might find him in a boxing gym or hauling a ruck in the forests of Kentucky.

ABOUT CIDER MILL PRESS
BOOK PUBLISHERS

Good ideas ripen with time. From seed to harvest, Cider Mill Press brings fine reading, information, and entertainment together between the covers of its creatively crafted books. Our Cider Mill bears fruit twice a year, publishing a new crop of titles each spring and fall.

"Where Good Books Are Ready for Press"
501 Nelson Place
Nashville, Tennessee 37214

cidermillpress.com